EXPLAINING THE LECTIONARY
FOR READERS

Abbatissae Sororibusque Franciscanis apud Arkley

Thomas O'Loughlin

Explaining the Lectionary for Readers

the columba press

First published in 2008 by
the columba press
55A Spruce Avenue, Stillorgan Industrial Park,
Blackrock, Co Dublin

Cover by Bill Bolger
Origination by The Columba Press
Printed in Ireland by ColourBooks Ltd, Dublin

ISBN 978 1 85607 603 6

Acknowledgement

I would like to acknowledge the help and feedback I have had from so
many people – mainly readers – to what is in this book. I would also like
to thank Dr Francisca Rumsey of the Poor Clare Monastery in Arkley,
and at the same time my colleague here in the Department in Lampeter,
for proofreading the manuscript.

Table of Contents

Preface

Dear Reader,

One of the incidental duties of most theologians is responding to requests from time to time to go and address a parish group on some aspect of Christian faith. What one is asked to speak about is often focused on helping the community explore some part of the Bible, and when one gets there the actual group who have gathered is made up of people who are already engaged in various ways with the Scriptures: they are members of a Bible Study group, a group that meets for reflection and uses Scripture as its basic resource, or they play an active part in the community's liturgy. If the community inviting one to speak is Catholic, then one can bet on two things: (1) that many in the group are readers at the Eucharist; and (2) there will be a warm welcome for anything one does in explaining the purpose and structure of the eucharistic lectionary. In those invitations lie the origins of this book.

Over the years I have noticed that the same questions come up repeatedly from groups of readers, and that there is interest around two central themes: (1) why do we bother with some or all of the readings? and (2) why do readings come up when they do? I hope those questions and, in particular, those two themes are addressed in this book. I have also found that simply explaining how the lectionary is structured (such items as the three-year cycle) gave the readers a sense of having a map that allowed them to know where their particular task or the reading of a certain text fitted into larger landscape of the liturgy. So providing a map of the Liturgy of the Word is this book's aim.

Once we have a sense of the overall structure and direction of the Liturgy of the Word, then we are in a better position to appreciate its deeper spiritual significance for us as individuals and as members of the church. The *General Instruction on the Lectionary* expressed that in these words:

That word constantly proclaimed in the liturgy is always a living, active word (see Hebrews 4:2) through the power of the Holy Spirit. It expresses the Father's love that never fails in its effectiveness towards us (n. 4).

And it is my hope that this book will help readers to see what they do as collaborating in this work of the Spirit.

By the way, there is an added, incidental value to this book: readers can use it to look up in their own Bibles the texts they are due to read at the liturgy and make themselves familiar with the text in plenty of time. Even if the translation in your Bible at home is different from the lectionary, it is of no importance because one of the best ways to appreciate the nuances of any text written in a foreign language – even if one has a command of Greek – is to read it in several translations, noting how the force of the words you read shifts slightly from translation to translation.

So, reader, I hope this book will help you understand a little more the task you have volunteered to perform, and to appreciate a little more the ministry in which you have been called to serve.

T.O'L
Lampeter
1 September 2007
Feast of St Verena

CHAPTER ONE

Some basics

This chapter's purpose is to address a few basic questions:
- Who is this book aimed at?
- Why do we have readings at the Eucharist?
- What do we mean by terms like 'Scripture', 'the Bible', and 'the Word of God'?
- What is a lectionary?

WHO IS THIS BOOK AIMED AT?

Those who regularly read the Word of God during the liturgy
It is the experience of most people who take part in the liturgy to have at some stage been asked to 'read' something. This may have been as short an item as a bidding prayer such as 'That the Lord will grant healing to the sick; Lord hear us,' or it may have been a long reading from the Book of Genesis with plenty of difficult sounding names. It may have been at a celebration for a special group, such as a class in school or in a ward in a hospital, or it may have been at some special occasion such as the wedding or funeral of a relative. It may also have been at the regular celebration of the Eucharist in a parish on a weekday or a Sunday, when people are called upon take a lead in the worship and prayer of their own community by reading from the Word. These people who are regularly called upon to read as part of the liturgy – often referred to as 'the readers' – form an important group in every Christian community for they have volunteered their energy and talents to serve their sisters and brothers in celebrating the weekly event that is the centre and summit of the Christian life and which transforms us from being

a collection of individuals into the Body of Christ. If this service is well done, it will build up the faith of the whole community; if it is badly done, then the experience of the liturgy is impoverished for all concerned. 'Good celebrations foster and nourish faith; poor celebrations weaken and destroy faith.'[1]

It is at this group, the readers, namely those who are called upon regularly to read the Word of God at the Eucharist in their communities, that this book is aimed. I hope also that it will be of use in two other ways: first, it will give all who are involved in planning the liturgy for a community an overview of the plan and design of the Liturgy of the Word over the various cycles found in the lectionary; second, in more elaborate courses on the nature of the liturgy, or in special training courses for readers, that it might serve as a handy guide for looking over the patterns that can be found in the lectionary but which can be all too easy to miss when one looks through the lectionary and has to turn pages and pages and pages.

What this book is not
Anyone who takes on the service of helping to unfold the mystery of Christ to her/his sisters and brothers should recognise that this requires both talents and training. The *General Instruction on the Lectionary* indeed presents this need in lofty terms:

> The preparation of readers must above all be spiritual, but what may be called 'technical preparation' is also needed. The spiritual preparation presupposes at least a biblical and liturgical formation. The purpose of their biblical formation is to give readers the ability to understand the readings in context and to perceive by the light of faith the central point of the revealed message. The liturgical formation ought to equip the readers to have some grasp of the meaning and structure of the liturgy of the word and of the significance of its connection with the liturgy of the eucharist. The technical

---

1. US Bishops' Committee on Liturgy (1972) *Music in Catholic Worship*, Washington, 6.

preparation should make the readers more skilled in the art of reading publicly, either with the power of their own voice or with the help of sound equipment.[2]

This little book is not a substitute for either a proper course of study of the content of the Scriptures, nor does it aim to explain the nature of the liturgy and the place of Scripture within it. Its aim is to provide a basic overview of how the readings are arranged in the lectionary over the three-year cycle. The hope is that once a reader recognises the elaborate structure of what is set before the People of God in the lectionary, that reader will want to engage further with her/his ministry and seek out the training and formation that is appropriate to his/her task in the Sunday assembly.

What this book can do
Someone who reads at the Eucharist every second or third Sunday can easily think that the whole business of the readings is a big jumble! One week it is a reading from the First Book of the Kings, the next week it is from the Book of the Apocalypse, and the next week it is from the Book of Leviticus. And, on the Sundays that the reader is not herself or himself reading it is hard to remember what the previous week's reading was, and the current week's reading seems to be from some even more obscure place such as the Book of Ecclesiasticus – and one wonders if that is the same as the Book of Wisdom or the Book of Sirach! Meeting the Liturgy of the Word one day at a time and with those occasions separated by a week means that getting any sense of there being a structure in the whole business is well nigh impossible.

Yet there is a structure. Indeed, the lectionary produced by the Catholic Church after the Second Vatican Council (1962-5) is the most formally organised and structured lectionary that has ever been produced by any church. So well thought out is that structure – as we shall see as we go through this book – that it

---

2. *General Instruction on the Lectionary*, 55.

has been adopted either wholly or with some adaptations by any number of western churches whose origins lie in the sixteenth-century Reformation.

Psychologists have found that any activity that can be broken into little bits will be done much better, in each little bit, if those engaged in the activity do not simply know the little bit they are working on, but have a grasp of the larger scene within which their little bits fit. Imagine there are three people painting plastic pipes of differing shapes in different colours. None knows what these pipes are to be used for or whether or not the work of the three painters fits together: the result is a sense of being disempowered, mere drudges, and the quality of the work will be indifferent. Now, show the three painters how the pipes fit together to make something beautiful and useful. The glimpse of the overall pattern is sufficient to transform their work. It can now be done both with greater satisfaction and efficiency: each little bit will be done better because it is seen as just one brick in a great edifice.

This need for an understanding of the overall structure of the lectionary was recognised from the outset by those who created it:

> The first requirement for one who is to preside over the celebration is a thorough knowledge of the structure of the Order of Readings so that he will know how to inspire good effects in the hearts of the faithful. Through study and prayer he must also develop a full understanding of the coordination and connection of the various texts of the Liturgy of the Word, so that the Order of Readings will become the source of a sound understanding of the mystery of Christ and his saving work.[3]

However, while the compilers of the lectionary thought that only priests needed to have an understanding of the structure of the choice of readings over the liturgical year, experience has shown that every reader is able to perform her/his ministry

---

3. *General Instruction on the Lectionary*, 39.

with greater skill, effect, and satisfaction if he/she can see the overall pattern of which the reading she/he is doing on a particular day is just one element.

So the purpose of this book is to provide everyone who ministers in the Liturgy of the Word with an overview of the structure of the whole three-year lectionary.

WHY DO WE HAVE READINGS AT THE EUCHARIST?

A reading from a gospel

From the very beginning, Christians have gathered to celebrate the Lord's meal which united them to one another in Christ, and so made them a people offering prayer and thanksgiving to the Father. At these meals the memory of Jesus was recalled for it was his presence, his words, his teaching about the Father that constituted them as a community: they recalled his words and deeds and this process of recollection at these gatherings became what we call 'the gospels'. Committed to writing, these retellings of the deeds and words of Jesus became the formative identity of the communities as they handed on to one another the good news. To belong to the community was to become part of the tradition of the community that reached back to the very first gatherings around Jesus while he was living with us. The tradition now reaches down to the community we become on Sunday morning and reaches outwards to every other such gathering. In these gatherings, by the early second century, the retelling of the good news by four early preachers – Mark, Matthew, John and Luke – gradually became the norm. To hear again those four accounts was to encounter the memory of the whole church. Therefore, now as then, whenever his People gather we recall the good news, and we do this (in the manner established by the second century[4]) by hearing again parts of the gospels of John, Mark, Matthew and Luke. They, then as now,

---

4. See M. Hengel (2000), *The Four Gospels and the One Gospel of Jesus Christ*, Harrisburg PA.

help unfold the mystery of Christ. Therefore, at every celebration of the Eucharist we have a reading from one of the four gospels.

A reading from the Old Testament
When the first Christians proclaimed their faith in Jesus as the Lord they did so by showing how what had happened in the life, death, and resurrection of Jesus happened 'according to the Scriptures'. In this action they adopted the notion of the Scriptures from their fellow Jews and give it a new significance among the followers of Jesus. Jesus and his deeds and words constituted 'the new relationship' with God (and for the word 'relationship' one can read 'covenant' or 'testament'), and it was prepared for, anticipated, promised during the time of 'the former relationship' (and for 'former' one can read 'older' or 'old'). So they continued to read the books that Jews at the time referred to as 'the law and the prophets' or as 'the scriptures.' We see this in accounts of early preaching and in the memories of the deeds of Jesus. Paul expressed this elegantly at the beginning of the Letter to the Romans: 'Paul, a servant of Jesus Christ, called to be an apostle, set apart for the gospel of God which he promised beforehand through his prophets in the holy scriptures, the gospel concerning his Son, who was descended from David according to the flesh and designated Son of God in power according to the Spirit of holiness by his resurrection from the dead, Jesus Christ our Lord' (Rom 1:1-4). To preach the gospel of Jesus one needs to be aware of what was promised in the holy scriptures – meaning those books (e.g. Isaiah or Jeremiah) that we refer to colloquially as 'the Old Testament'. And these scriptures became something that the church valued as containing the Word of God and as indispensable if any community or individual were to appreciate Jesus as the one who fulfils the 'law and the prophets'. So we recall Jesus's action: 'And he came to Nazareth, where he had been brought up, and he went to the synagogue, as his custom was, on the Sabbath day. And he stood up to read, and there was given to him the

book of the prophet Isaiah. He opened the book and found the place where it was written, "The Spirit of the Lord is upon me, because he has anointed me to preach good news to the poor. He has sent me to proclaim release to the captives and recovering of sight to the blind, to set at liberty those who are oppressed, to proclaim the acceptable year of the Lord." And he closed the book, and gave it back to the attendant, and sat down, and the eyes of all in the synagogue were fixed on him. And he began to say to them, "Today this scripture has been fulfilled in your hearing"' (Lk 4:16-21). Peter, preaching the coming of Jesus among the people, appeals both to the prophet Joel and the psalms of David (Acts 2:14-37): their words allow us to understand what happened in the life and death of Jesus. And in recognising the risen Christ at Emmaus the disciples discovered from Jesus the full meaning of 'the scriptures': 'And Jesus said to them, "O foolish men, and slow of heart to believe all that the prophets have spoken! Was it not necessary that the Christ should suffer these things and enter into his glory?" And beginning with Moses and all the prophets, he interpreted to them in all the scriptures the things concerning himself' (Lk 24:25-7). Hence there has been a conviction among Christians down the centuries – expressed in the Creed in the phrase 'On the third day he rose again in accordance with the Scriptures' – that the Old Testament must be valued as the Word of God and as helping us unfold the mystery of Christ. Therefore, at our gatherings for the Eucharist – and virtually always at our Sunday gatherings – we read passages from the older testament, which we refer to as the 'first reading and the psalm'.

A reading from an early church letter
From the very beginning the communities that had sprung up from the preaching of the apostles recognised that they were not just local churches, but were parts of a whole new people that reached from one end of the earth to the other. This larger sense of belonging to the whole church was fostered by visiting one another and by exchanging letters which were read in commu-

nity after community. These communications helped form the individual communities in The Way of Jesus and gave them a common sense of belonging. We glimpse this sending and receiving and exchanging of letters in this line in the letter to the church at Colossae: 'And when this letter has been read among you, have it read also in the church of the Laodiceans; and see that you read also the letter from Laodicea' (Col 4:16). Among all the letters that circulated – and only a fraction has survived – those linked with the names of Paul, Peter, James, John, and Jude came to be seen as having an authority as coming from the first generation of preachers, and these continued to be treasured and heard again at assemblies of the churches. Therefore, at virtually every Eucharistic gathering today we read a passage from these early Christian teachers, and often refer to it as 'the epistle' or 'the second reading'.

Concentric circles
So we can think of the readings at the Eucharist as a series of concentric circles:
- at the centre is the gospel which is a recollection and celebration of the mystery of Jesus, the Anointed One;
- this recollection is given added dimensions by readings from the Old Testament: the Law (such as Genesis or Exodus), the prophets (such as Amos or Joel), the Psalms, and the Writings (such as the Book of Wisdom or the Books of the Maccabees);
- then there are the readings of the great early Christian teachers' letters to churches, such as those of Paul.

The purpose of the readings is that, in the words of the *General Instruction on the Lectionary*, in accordance with ancient practice there should be a 're-establishing [of] the use of Scripture in every celebration of the liturgy' and that this should be seen as 'the unfolding mystery of Christ' being 'recalled during the course of the liturgical year'.[5]

---

5. *General Instruction on the Lectionary*, 1 and 3.

Old Testament and Gospel

It should now have become clear that there is a special link between the first reading from the Old Testament and the gospel each Sunday. The *General Instruction* describes the place of the gospel thus:

> The reading of the gospel is the high point of the Liturgy of the Word. For this the other readings, in their established sequence from the Old and New Testament, prepare the assembly.[6]

However, for most Sundays each year (whether during the seasons such as Lent, and always in Ordinary Time) the reading that is related to the gospel is that from the Old Testament.

This immediately raises the question about how we approach these readings. In the liturgy we use an approach that can already be found in the earliest Christian preaching – as we have already seen above looking at the opening of Paul's letter to the Romans – whereby the Old Testament is seen to prepare for the coming of Jesus among his people to inaugurate the New Covenant. This approach among the first churches was summed up in one sentence by the man who wrote the letter to the Hebrews: 'In many and various ways God spoke of old to our fathers by the prophets; but in these last days he has spoken to us by a Son, whom he appointed the heir of all things, through whom also he created the world' (Heb 1:1-2). This perspective for reading the books of the Old Testament is expressed by the *General Instruction* thus:

> When in celebrating the liturgy the Church proclaims both the Old and New Testament, it is proclaiming the one and the same mystery of Christ.
>
> The New Testament lies hidden in the Old; the Old Testament comes fully to life in the New. Christ himself is the centre and fullness of all of Scripture, as he is of the entire liturgy.[7]

---

6. *General Instruction on the Lectionary*, 13.
7. *General Instruction on the Lectionary*, 5.

It is important to note that this perspective on the Old Testament is one that is related directly to faith in Jesus as the Christ and in the relationship of the church to him. It is not the same perspective on those ancient texts that is used in most studies of those texts in biblical and theological courses, where the primary focus of investigation is on the meaning of a text in its original context rather than in any later use of that text. It is useful to keep these distinct perspective in mind: what we do in a Scripture Studies Group or a Biblical Studies Course is not what we are doing when read recall these texts in the liturgy. Both approaches are important and can be complementary, but if they are confused the result can lead to muddle. The classic muddle is when someone explains an Old Testament reading at the Eucharist in terms of what it meant in an agrarian temple-treasury culture in the Ancient Near East and many people wonder why we bother with such stuff to try to make sense of believing in the good news today. Alternatively, someone hears a reading from Isaiah during Advent, and the homily explores this in terms of the coming of Jesus two thousand years ago, now in the community celebrating, and at the End of time, and thinks that this is just 'dodgy exegesis' because it is so different from the approach in a scripture class. In the one case we are trying to make sense of a text in its historical context; in the other, the mystery of God's self-revelation to humanity. These endeavours are not in conflict, and should be complementary.

Implications
If the readings at the Eucharist are there to help unfold the mystery of Jesus Christ, then several important consequences flow from this:
- We are not reading the Scriptures simply to get a knowledge of the Bible.
- We are not reading these passages because many Christians consider reading the Bible a valuable activity in itself.
- This action is not part of a Bible Study, nor should it resemble the classroom atmosphere of a study group.

- The focus of all our reading is not an abstract understanding of the scriptural text – such as would be carried out by a biblical exegete in a theology course – but to see what each portion of text (whether from the gospel, the Old Testament, the psalm, or the epistle) reveals to us about the Paschal Mystery.
- Our reading is not book-focused; it is not text-focused; it is focused on Jesus as the Christ.
- The gospel is the primary focus on the mystery of the Christ in each celebration; the Old Testament and Psalm relate to it as background, example, context, or elaboration; the epistle is a separate attempt to focus on the mystery of the Christ through the help of early Christian teachers.
- The readings are to help us encounter the person of Jesus Christ in whose presence and name we have gathered.

'The word of God unceasingly calls to mind and extends the plan of salvation, which achieves its fullest expression in the liturgy. The liturgical celebration becomes therefore the continuing, complete, and effective presentation of God's word.'[8]

A Basic Principle of the Lectionary
We can now state a fundamental principle of the lectionary for Sundays:

1. The centre of every Liturgy of the Word will be the mystery of the Christ as exemplified in a gospel passage;

2. To this will be linked a reading from the Old Testament – and we read the passage from the perspective of it helping us Christians to understand the aspect of the mystery of Christ found in the gospel passage of the day;

3. There will usually be a reading from an epistle, but for most of the year (Ordinary Time) it will have no direct link to that Sunday's gospel (and consequently it will not have a link to the preceding Old Testament reading).

---

8. *General Instruction on the Lectionary*, 4.

WHAT DO WE MEAN BY TERMS LIKE 'SCRIPTURE', 'THE BIBLE,' AND 'THE WORD OF GOD'?

One matter that causes a lot of confusion for readers is the range of terms that are used in referring to material that is read at the Eucharist. The confusion arises from two sources. First, the fact that the different terms have come into use over the centuries in relation to the sacred books of the Christians and each has a particular nuance that means it is favoured by one group more than another or in one situation more than another. Second, all the terms seem to relate to the same 'stuff' than can be found in a book, bound between two covers, that one can buy in a shop with the title 'The Holy Bible' written in big letters on the cover. So, some people ask, what's the problem?

To try to clear up this matter, and show the nuances of each term, here is a list of terms:

Scripture. This is a term that was already in use by the very first generation of Christians: for example in Luke's gospel we hear that Jesus 'began to say to them, "Today this scripture has been fulfilled in your hearing"' (Lk 4:21). But as it is used today it refers to a particular part of the memory of Christians relating to the texts that have been valued by Christians as being foundational for their understanding of their faith. A basic usage of this term can be seen in 2 Tim 3:16: 'All scripture is inspired by God and profitable for teaching, for reproof, for correction, and for training in righteousness.'

The Scriptures. Again this term has been in use since the beginning of Christianity (e.g. Mt 21:42; Lk 24:45; 1 Cor 15:3) when it was used to refer to the collection of writings that were held to be sacred, i.e. 'Scripture', in many forms of Judaism that existed at the time. Among those groups the extent of what was considered to be 'the Scriptures' varied, as well as the importance that should be attached to them. The Christians took their position from those forms of Judaism that held that category of 'the Scriptures' included a wide range of texts: the pentateuch (the first five books attributed to Moses), the prophets, other books written in Hebrew, along with more recent books written originally in Greek. The Christians also took over an attitude that those texts, 'the Scriptures,' were of great significance in understanding the unfolding of God's purposes in history leading up to the life, death and resurrection of Jesus.

This term became the most widely used Christian designation of the collection of holy books. And, by the end of the second century the texts (e.g. the letters of Paul and four gospels) produced by the first generations of Christians, and used in the liturgy, were also being included under the designation 'the Scriptures'.

So when we meet the term 'the Scriptures' in any of the books of the New Testament, it refers to the Old Testament as adopted by the Christians. When we use the term 'the Scriptures' in general conversation today, we mean both the Old Testament and the New Testament.

The Bible. This term really is best kept to refer to an object, a book that one can buy in a shop. The book is an anthology of texts some of which are designated by Christians as the 'Old Testament' and some as the 'New Testament'. The exact number of texts that make up this book varies between the different Christian groups. Eastern Orthodox Bibles contain a few more texts than Catholic Bibles, and Catholic Bibles contain more texts than the Bibles preferred by many Protestant communities.[9]

As a rule of thumb, groups who use the term 'the Bible' often are interested in the whole book as a collection for private reading and that reading, whether done alone or in a group, is a religious activity in its own right. Such reading of 'the Bible' (collectively or individually) is a distinct activity to using 'the Scriptures' as a part of the liturgy as that is understood by Catholics. One of the difficulties some Protestant churches have with the Catholic lectionary is that their standard weekly act of worship is focused on reading the Bible as a religious end in itself, then trying to understand it, and then using the text as the basis of praise or petition. In the normal Catholic assembly, it is the community meal that is the focus, and reading these ancient texts is

9. This will be explained in more detail in chapter 13.

done to promote memory and understanding not of the text but of the event of which the text is but a recollection in writing. This can be seen in practice in many Protestant liturgies: the reading is read from a Bible that is suitably marked with the day's reading (and hence it is introduced by giving the chapter and verse to set the context), while in Catholic liturgies the reading is done from a special book and the focus is on the particular piece of text being read (hence it is introduced simply as 'A reading from the Book of Exodus' but there is no statement like 'from the fifth chapter beginning at the first verse'). These little shifts in practice and terminology are symptomatic of far more deep-seated differences in how the Scriptures have been received, used, and understood in the different traditions.

The Word of God. This phrase is used to refer to the whole communication of God to humanity as a life-giving event in the Holy Spirit. This is the dynamic reality of encountering the Father's communication with us in Jesus, the Christ, who is the Word and who sends the Spirit into human minds, hearts and imaginations to lead us further on the way to the truth. The Father bids us to enter into his rest, the fullness of life, and (as the Letter to the Hebrews puts it): 'Let us therefore strive to enter that rest, that no one fall by the same sort of disobedience. For the word of God is living and active, sharper than any two-edged sword, piercing to the division of soul and spirit, of joints and marrow, and discerning the thoughts and intentions of the heart' (Heb 4:11-2). It is this communication of God that we encounter in the whole of the liturgy, and in one particular way in the Liturgy of the Word, and hence the readings are concluded with the phrase 'The word of the Lord' or 'This is the word of the Lord.' However, when we use this phrase we are referring to a spiritual encounter; we are not using a pious synonym for 'the scriptures'.

The New Testament.

The Old Testament.

The New Covenant.

The Old Covenant. These four terms have to be understood together. Most of the time we use the related phrases 'The New
Testament' and 'The Old Testament' to refer to the major divisions of the Christian Bible. The New Testament refers to the
books written by the first followers of Jesus which came to be
understood as Scripture by Christians during the first century
and half. Then by contrast, all the earlier writings that date from
before the time of the church go to make up the 'Old Testament'.

However, the original meaning of these phrases is quite different, and that original use explains why we refer to these parts
as 'testaments' rather than use clearer terms such as 'the
Christian Books' and the 'Pre-Christian Books'.

A 'testament' (from the Latin *testamentum* translating the
word *diathéké* used by Paul, Luke and the author of Hebrews) is
the word for the relationship that is established by the Christ between us his people and the Father. So in accounts of the
Eucharist in Paul (1 Cor 11:25) and Luke (22:20) Jesus refers to
the new relationship that is established in his blood between
those who share in his cup, and the Father. We now tend to us
the phrase 'the new covenant' for this relationship. Once the relationship that Jesus had established came to be known as 'the
new testament', then it was almost automatic that the relationship between God and his people that existed before Jesus
would be called 'the old testament'. Later, the scriptural books
which recall the relationship established by Jesus came to be
known as 'the books of the new testament'; and, similarly, 'the
books of the old testament'. Then in time this became shorthand
as names for collections of books. So today, we use 'Old
Testament' and 'New Testament' as names for collections of
books, while keeping the word 'covenant' for the relationship.
However, when we use the terms 'Old Testament' and 'New
Testament' we should keep in mind that we are not just referring to books, but to the way we look at them.

The Good News.

The Gospel.

The Gospels. These three terms need to be looked at together. The announcement of the story of the life, teaching, death and resurrection of Jesus has constituted the unique centre of all Christian preaching (the whole of the preaching is often referred to as the *kerugma*). This central core is known as the 'good news' or 'the gospel' which are attempts to render the Greek word *euangelion* which means, literally, something like 'good announcement.'

By 'the gospels' we mean those four early versions (linked with Mark, Luke, Matthew, and John) of 'the gospel' – the story of Jesus – which gained rapid authority in virtually every church by the mid-second century, to such an extent that the many other gospels that were in use (see Lk 1:1) disappeared from being heard in public in the liturgy.

The Hebrew Bible. This refers to the collection of texts, each of which is considered to belong to the Scriptures, for which we have an ancient text in the Hebrew language. This is a technical term in biblical studies – and in some discussions of the extent of the canon – but it is sometimes used as if it is simply a more de-nominationally neutral term for what Christians refer to as the Old Testament. This usage is both sloppy and inaccurate. The Christian Old Testament includes all the texts that are to be found in the Hebrew Bible, but the Old Testament includes (for most Christians, and certainly for the Catholic liturgy) many other books that are not found in the Hebrew Bible. Moreover, when most Christians use those texts in the liturgy, they do not read them either as ancient religious texts or as bearers of a sacred message in and of themselves, but in so far as they are the Old Testament and come to full meaning in the context of the gospel (as we have already noted above).

WHAT IS A LECTIONARY?

A lectionary is book that presents the contents of the Scriptures in such a way that portions of text can be read on particular days, for particular events, or in particular situations. A lect-ionary could be as simple as a list of references which could then be looked up in a Bible, the beginning and end of the appointed portion marked, and then the reading read from there. However, for convenience these portions are better printed as such, and then arranged in sequences with all the readings (Old Testament, psalm, epistle, gospel) for a particular liturgy all gathered in one place.

Sometimes the lectionary is further divided into books for the use of various readers, and it is common to find the gospels gathered into one book so that there is an elaborate 'Book of the Gospels' that can be carried into the assembly in procession.[10] While such books are most important, to go into the details of their arrangement, or the history of lectionaries, would take us too far from our purpose.[11]

10. The *General Instruction on the Lectionary*, 17 and 113 lays great stress on the importance of having a Book of the Gospels for use in the Sunday liturgy, and having, in addition, other special books (which are sub-sections of the lectionary) for the various ministers who announce the word of God.

11. There are pointers to where this information can be obtained in chapter 15.

CHAPTER TWO

Structures within the Lectionary

To get an idea of how the lectionary is structured we have to look at these five questions:
- The structure of the liturgical year
- How lectionaries can be compiled
- How the lectionary conveys the differing christologies of the evangelists
- How which year of the lectionary is to be read is determined
- What exactly do we mean by 'ordinary time.'

THE STRUCTURE OF THE LITURGICAL YEAR

The lectionary is arranged to provide readings from Scripture for every day of the year. So the basic structure of the lectionary is determined by the structure of the liturgical year.

The liturgical year is made up of two kinds of time:

Festival Time

There are two periods of festival time:

1. Advent and Christmas: when we celebrate the preparation for the coming of the Christ – which we call Advent – and the celebration of the fact that he has come among us, his birth, and the significance of God being with us in Jesus – which we call Christmas.

2. Lent and Easter: when we prepare to welcome new members into the church and seek to renew our own discipleship – which we call Lent – and the time when we celebrate the central mystery of faith – Holy Week and Easter Sunday – and the celebration of the period of the Risen Christ among us – Eastertime which ends with Pentecost.

Ordinary Time

This is all the rest of the year when we continue to reflect on the life and teaching of Jesus, aware that he has come among us (the mystery of Christmas) and aware that he is the Risen One who stands among us in the church (the mystrey of Easter). What exactly we mean by 'ordinary time' will be examined in the last section of this chapter.

Cutting across the whole year is another distinction in our celebration of time: the distinction between the Day of the Lord, Sunday, and the rest of the week: weekdays. In traditional Christian understanding Sunday is always special, it is the day when we gather as a community, celebrate the Risen Christ's presence in a special way, and rejoice and rest because we are a people loved and redeemed. This understanding of Sunday is quite distant from the experience of most people today when Sunday is part of the weekend, it is 'time off', and time for fun and play with family and friends rather than for thinking of the community. This dissonance between the way the liturgy views Sunday and how people think of it is one of the pastoral difficulties of our time. To see this difference in perception between the 'official' view of Sunday and our own, just read this sentence:

> The church celebrates the paschal mystery on the first day of the week, known as the Lord's Day or Sunday. This follows a tradition handed down from the Apostles, which took its origin from the day of Christ's resurrection. Thus Sunday should be considered the original feast day.[1]

However, while we must acknowledge this dissonance between how Sunday was viewed traditionally and how we experience it, unless we are prepared to take on board this aspect of Christian tradition as part of our view of time we cannot understand why (1) this is the day on which we gather, and (2) the level of significance that the lectionary gives to Sundays.

The core of the liturgical year can be seen as composed of these 'kinds' of days, and the lectionary has to provide readings for every one of them:

1. *General Norms of the Liturgical Year and the Calendar*, n. 4.

Advent / Sundays	Advent / Weekdays
The Feast of Christmas	
Christmas Season / Sundays	Christmas Season / Weekdays
Lent / Sundays	Lent / Weekdays
Holy Week and Easterday	
Eastertime / Sundays	Eastertime / Weeksdays
Ordinary Time / Sundays	Ordinary Time / Weekdays

In addition, the lectionary has to provide readings for:

Special Feasts (e.g. Corpus Christi or Trinity Sunday)
The year's saints' days (only a few have special readings)
Celebrations of the Eucharist on special occasions

So, in order to learn more about the lectionary we have to look at its contents under the headings of the different kinds of day over the course of the year for which it has to provide readings. These will be examined in turn in:

- The readings for Advent and Christmas in chapter 3.
- The readings for Lent and Easter in chapter 4.
- The Sunday readings for Ordinary Time in chapters 5 (Year A: Matthew); 6 (Year B: Mark); and 7 (Year C: Luke).
- The Weekday readings for Ordinary Time in chapter 8.
- The readings for other celebrations in chapter 9.

HOW LECTIONARIES ARE COMPILED

Clearly, it is a simple task to pick readings for celebrations like Christmas Day (read some or all of the infancy narratives in Matthew or Luke), or Good Friday (read the account of the crucifixion from one of the gospels) or Pentecost (read the account in the Acts of the Apostles). But what would you choose for a Sunday in July or August, or a weekday in October? Finding an answer to this question has exercised the minds of Christians down the centuries.

1. Seasons, themes, and continuous reading

In the history of Christian lectionaries there have been two ways of creating lectionaries. The first, and simplest, is to opt for continuous reading (*lectio continua*) of texts as this allows biblical books to be appreciated whole, and it avoids any 'temptation' to skip over bits that are unpleasant. Pick a day as the starting point and decree that on that day we begin reading either a gospel, a book of the Old Testament, or an epistle, and then keep going, day after day, or Sunday after Sunday, until the biblical book is finished. Then start on another biblical book. Given that the gospels – and these will always be the driving force in the readings for our gatherings for the Eucharist – are episodic in structure, this method is ideally suited to appreciating them: read one story / incident today, then move to the next tomorrow or next Sunday. Such lectionaries are known as 'continuous-reading lectionaries'.

However, given that the liturgical year is fundamental to Christian liturgy – a component of practice already established by the time the Acts of the Apostles was written – the method of continuous reading can never hold unrivalled sway. How could one read a parable text on Easter Day just because it was the next reading in a sequence? The very fact that the rudiments of the liturgical year predate the gospels we possess has meant that the nature of the day – for example, if today is the day of Pentecost – determines the reading if there is a reading that is linked to that day. So at Christmas we need to hear of Bethlehem; at Easter of the resurrection; and on 6 August of the transfiguration. Such lectionaries using readings appropriate to the time being celebrated are known as 'eclogadic lectionaries'.

Alongside these two major dynamics in creating lectionaries there is a third, lesser, factor: the appropriateness of a particular scriptural passage to a celebration either of a saint or topic. Thus the Common of Doctors in the 1570 Missal had Mt 5:13-19 as its gospel, while the Mass in Time of War had Mt 24:3-8. As with eclogadic lectionaries, the choice of reading is being determined by what is being celebrated on that day. This reaches its logical conclusion in the readings at weddings, funerals, and other major celebrations; but the celebration of 'special Masses' often leads to choices whose 'fit' is tenuous or to superficial 'links' between a piece of text and a situation. However, given that the celebration is about a special event, and this has to be referred to in the homily, there is a certain inherent demand that one somehow finds a 'suitable' reading.

2. Ordinary Time

Although every lectionary has to have an eclogadic element (for Christmas and Easter at the very least), it is still desirable that as wide a range of texts as possible be used in the liturgy; hence the creation of any lectionary that covers the year has to be a compromise between the two selection methods.[2]

The compromise worked out for the 1970 Lectionary was complex, elaborate, and on a scale never before attempted in Christian liturgical history. It is this sophistication – once the inevitable need for a compromise is recognised – that has recommended it to so many groups in their several searches for a lectionary. So on certain days in the year when key moments in the Christ-event are to be celebrated, the readings are the same each and every year: the Passion according to John in the Good Friday Liturgy is the best example. Then there are the eclogadic choices for Christmas and Easter, and to a lesser extent for Lent and for Advent: but varied over a cycle of three years for the Sundays and other major feasts. Then outside these special seasons we have 'ordinary time' and here the criterion is continuous reading and by spreading the material over the three-year cycle a greater variety of gospel material is now used than ever before. The simple device of using Matthew in year A, Mark in B, and Luke in C, now seems so obvious that we forget that it

---

2. In terms of planned liturgical time, the third method can be ignored as it would destroy the whole rationale of a lectionary: thus the current lectionary's assumption that on saints' feasts – very special festivals excepted – the readings 'of the day' rather than those from the Commons are used.

was a revolution in 1970. Today one has to speak to groups who have just adopted the lectionary to hear expressions of 'what a brilliant idea' it is to devote a year to each of the three synoptics (knowing that John is well represented in the seasons' sections). For most people, this is about as much as they know about the structure of the lectionary in Ordinary Time: each year we read one evangelist. Is there anything more to be said?

DIFFERENT EVANGELISTS: DIFFERENT CHRISTOLOGIES

To appreciate the lectionary we must note that once the option of continuous reading was taken, there were still many other decisions as to what would and would not be included in the continuous reading. There were three key factors facing the selectors: (1) that even in Mark – once the chapters after 11:1, relating to the final week in Jerusalem are omitted since they are used in Lent / Holy Week – there is too much material to distribute over the available number of Sundays unless very large sections (often made up of several stories) were read each Sunday; (2) there are passages in 'the triple tradition' (where Matthew and Luke are reformulating material in Mark) so alike each other that they would be given undue prominence and *de facto* be read each year, and so these have to be curtailed; and (3) there are parts of each gospel text that for a variety of reasons are so problematic (e.g. corrupt texts, duplications, interpolations) that they are best omitted from public reading or pruned of erratic verses. Hence the selectors describe their work in the 1981 edition not as 'continuous reading' but more precisely as 'semi-continuous'.

If we take Mark as an example we have 'continuous reading' up to the time Jesus arrives in Jerusalem and then some snippets from the Jerusalem discourses. The result was that the selectors had a total of 405 verses[3] from between Mk 1:1 and 10:52 avail-

---

3. Using Nestle-Aland's numbering in the Greek text which, in effect, stands behind our translations rather than Vatican *editio typica* of the Clementine-Vulgate or the two editions of the *Nova Vulgata* (1979 and 1986): the 1969 *Ordo Lectionum* provided only text references, while the *Nova Vulgata* has had almost no impact on the lectionary we use today.

able to them for Ordinary Time. However, they used only c. 190 of these (i.e. just under half the text), plus 20 verses from Mk 12-13, and 70 verses from John. This selection was not just a case of pruning and dividing out what was left: knowing that they had to select, they deliberately adopted a policy of presenting the pieces of the gospel as part of the larger plan to show the gospel writers' intentions. They assumed that each of the synoptics 'presents us with a recognisable' and, we might add, distinctive 'portrait of Christ and a *particular approach* [their italics] to his teaching.' Hence the gospels are presented separately over the three years.[4] Their aim in this process of selection was outlined as 'allowing the main lines of the structure and theology of each ... to be grasped by preacher and reader [which] should allow the message of each ... to penetrate gradually into the conscious-ness of the faithful'.[5] They then provided the three schemata they envisage acting as the scaffolding over each year. But then (possibly recognising that neither (1) what a text's audience hears is static over time or cultures, nor (2) does biblical scholar-ship stand still) they add that 'such schemes are not definitive, but it is hoped that they will be a help'.[6] Each scheme will be ex-amined in detail in the chapter of this book dealing with that part of the liturgical year.

We get a flavour of how these schemes work by taking Mark as an example. It declared that it sees Mark's 'main interest' as 'the person of Jesus himself'. This is seen as progressively revealed in the text as the journey towards Jerusalem moves forwards and is based around the climactic question 'Who do men say that I am?' (Mk 8:29). It sees Peter's 'You are the Christ' as at 'the heart of Mark's gospel'. In taking this position the lectionary is following the mainstream of contemporary exegetical thinking about Mark today – indeed since the lectionary appeared there has been an increased emphasis among scholars on the need to view each gospel as an entire unit as opposed to seeing them as

---

4. See Introduction to the Lectionary, 1982, p. xlvii.
5. See Introduction to the Lectionary, 1982, p. xlvii.
6. See Introduction to the Lectionary, 1982, p. xlvii.

quarries for the traditions that lie behind our texts.[7] The
Lectionary then explains the inclusion of the 57 verses from John
on Sundays 17 to 21 as adopting a single unit from John's, 'sermon on the "Bread of Life"' which it sees as fitting 'well into [a
particular] part of Mark's gospel, which is concerned with Jesus'
revelation of himself and is known as "the Bread section".' And,
as dovetailing of texts goes, this is about as neat as anything we
might find: on Sunday 14 we have Mk 6:30-34 which is followed
in the gospel text (6:35-44) with the feeding miracle of the five
loaves and the two fish, which is supplanted in the liturgical
reading by the bread/feeding/eating sermon from John. The
compilers do not explain the rationale for selecting Jn 18:33b-37
for Christ the King, but this to my mind is rather pleasant for
while in mathematics consistency is virtue, in theology its sys-
tematic invocation often spells death to that imaginative process
without which faith is impossible.[8]

The scaffolding sees the 34 Sundays of Ordinary Time as
being divisible into three Units, each divided again into Stages,
and then with a key point for each Sunday's passage. So Mark is
read as revealing the figure of Jesus the Messiah (Unit 1), then
'the Mystery of Jesus' progressively revealed (Unit 2), and then
the Mystery of the Son of Man (Unit 3). Unit 2, for example, is
then seen as Jesus revealing himself to the Jewish crowds (Stage
1), then to his disciples (Stage 2), and then manifesting himself
(Stage 3). Then to take a Sunday within Stage 2, e.g. Sunday 11:
Mk 4:26-34, we have it described as 'Parables of the Kingdom'. It
is this keynote that then acts as the criterion for which snippet of
the Old Testament is chosen (Ezek 17:22-24) and thus the Psalm
(Ps 91:2-3, 13-16).

These structures can be studied in diagrams in the chapters
below.

---

7. See, for example, the essays in R. Bauckham ed., *The Gospels for All
Christians* (Grand Rapids, MI/Cambridge 1998).
8. Nor do they explain the choice of Jn 1:35-42 for Sunday 2.

WHICH YEAR OF THE LECTIONARY ARE WE IN?

The decision in 1970 to spread the lectionary for Sundays over a three-year cycle, and weekdays over a two-year cycle, made it necessary for every celebrant and reader to know which year in the cycle we are in. How is this determined?

Which gospel is read on Sundays in any calendar year is determined by the simple method of dividing the date by three: if the remainder is 1, then it is the first year of the cycle and the Year of Matthew; if the remainder is 2, then the second year and the Year of Mark; and, if the date is perfectly divisible, it is year 3, the Year of Luke.[9]

So, for example:

2006÷3=668 'and two over', hence it is 'year 2'.

2010÷3=670 'and nothing over', hence it is 'year 3'.

2023÷3=674 'and one over', hence it is 'year 1'.

For weekdays, the formula is even simpler: if the year is an odd number (e.g. 2007, 2009, 2011) then it is year 1 (which is an odd number); if it is even (e.g. 2008, 2010, 2012), then it is year 2 (an even number).

There is no need for a feat of memory or a special table: just a quick bit of division. From an ecumenical perspective this was an inspired way of determining the cycle as there is no 'Vatican inspired Year Zero' telling people that a particular year is Year A – it is simply a matter of AD and maths!

THE NOTION OF ORDINARY TIME

Let there be lights in the dome of the sky to separate the day from the night; and let them be for signs and for seasons and for days and years (Gen 1:14).

The phrase 'Ordinary Time' came into existence with the translation of the 1969 Missal into English where it was chosen as a translation of the Latin name for the time outside Advent-Christmas and Lent-Easter which is *Tempus per annum* (literally: 'the time during the year'). However, the phrase 'ordinary time'

---

9. See *General Instruction on the Lectionary*, 66, fn. 102.

is an excellent term to capture a most important aspect of ritual time: that there are differences in stress.

At the heart of any sense of time and ritual, time and religion, or time, calendars and memory is the alternation of *stressed* and *unstressed* time. Stressed time is the special occasion, that which is out of the ordinary, that which is marked aside for particular joyful celebration or special serious attention. In the modern secular year such stressed times would be the time for tax returns or the annual visit of the auditors or the 'Cup Final' or the week of a major sporting event. These are times that are not just any day, but known about, prepared for beforehand, and times when normal routine can be set aside. But if there are to be such special times, then there has to be unstressed time. When life becomes a perpetual holiday, you have no holidays!

The ordinary is, by contrast with the special times and notable events, the time when we just get on with the job. It is when there is 'nothing special happening' but also when we are acting 'normally'. So if we think of the two great festivals of the liturgy, Easter and Christmas, as the great events, then the time not connected with them is the ordinary time. It is this usage that gives rise to the phrase 'Sundays of Ordinary Time' and makes it such an appropriate designation.

We, as Christians, live in a complex calendar: over the course of the year there are stressed/unstressed times; but also over the course of the week there are stressed/unstressed times. In the annual cycles it is the difference between Lent-Easter with Advent-Christmas on the one hand, and all the rest of the time. Within the week, it is the difference between Sunday on the one hand, and the rest of the time on the other. So we give these Sundays of Ordinary Time special attention as the key day for Christians during the seven days that make up the week; but these Sundays are lesser affairs than those of the special seasons.

One of the tasks of those responsible for celebrating the liturgy is to have a sense of the balance of these days of differing ritual quality.

For everything there is a season, and a time for every matter
under heaven:
a time to be born, and a time to die;
a time to plant, and a time to pluck up what is planted;
a time to kill, and a time to heal;
a time to break down, and a time to build up;
a time to weep, and a time to laugh;
a time to mourn, and a time to dance;
a time to throw away stones, and a time to gather stones
together;
a time to embrace, and a time to refrain from embracing;
a time to seek, and a time to lose;
a time to keep, and a time to throw away;
a time to tear, and a time to sew;
a time to keep silence, and a time to speak;
a time to love, and a time to hate;
a time for war, and a time for peace (Qoh 3:1-8).

CHAPTER THREE

The Readings for Advent and Christmas

Christmas is our celebration of the mystery of the birth of Jesus the Lord. Like all great moments it needs both a time of preparation and a time to let it sink in: the time of preparation is Advent, the time to let it sink in is Christmastide. Together, the preparation and the time around and just after Christmas form the most recognisable period in the Christian year. Even people with only a very hazy notion about Christianity know that Christmas is a Christian feast, and while we Christians know that Easter is the greater feast, Christmas feels like the bigger event and it stands out for us more.

Once we had begun to celebrate Christmas, it was inevitable that we would have to have a 'run-up period' and thus we have Advent. Once we had Advent, it was inevitable that people would not just see it as a run-up, but would ask what it was 'for' – and so we have the various Advent themes such as recalling the time of the Old Covenant, recalling the waiting for the Anointed One, recalling our own sinfulness, and recalling that the Christ who came once in Bethlehem, comes among us today in the church in word and sacrament, and will come again at the end as the judge of the living and the dead. So the period of Advent is, liturgically, a 'theme-rich environment'.

The same happened with Christmas: once we were celebrating the birth of Jesus, and naturally we used the infancy gospels of Matthew and Luke as the core of our remembering, we began to celebrate all the events that are found surrounding the birth of Jesus. So we celebrated his circumcision 'on the eighth day' with a feast on 1 January, the coming of the Wise Men/Kings on the feast of the Epiphany, and later the feast of the presentation in the temple (2 February). So Christmastide is, liturgically, a 'memory rich environment'.

Then there are the odd celebrations that do not seem to fit in, but which have been absorbed into Christmas celebration, such as memorial of St Stephen on 26 December (this day is still called 'St Stephen's Day' in many countries and we recall that 'good' King Wenceslas looked out on it!) or the memorial of Pope Sylvester I (Bishop of Rome 314-335) on 31 December (which is known as 'Sylvestertag'/'Sylvesternacht' in Germany and has special customs under that name). The reason these are celebrated around Christmas is that they already had their place in the Christian calendar of celebrations before we began to celebrate Christmas as a feast.

It is these factors (themes in Advent, celebrations of events in Christmastide) that form the nature of the liturgy. The lectionary then tries to supply a range of suitable readings for these days.

However, since we have far more suitable readings for these themes and events than we could use in one year, we have a cycle of three years of readings.

The cycle of three years has the added advantage that it allows us to shift perspective on the mystery of the Lord's coming from year to year. This is of crucial importance for the church, for one of the characteristics of the mystery of the encounter of God and humanity in Jesus is that no matter how many ways we reflect on it, we will always discover within it new depths of what it means to us and its implications for how we live as Christians.

So the basic rule for understanding the lectionary in these seasons is: look at the time or event we are celebrating, the lectionary provides materials for our reflection on this day.

For Advent we can set these themes as follows:

Sundays			
	Gospel Theme	**Old Testament Theme**	**Epistle Theme**
First	The Lord's coming at the End of time	Prophesies about (a) the Messiah [the Christ] and (b) about the Messianic Age.	Exhortations and proclamations of the various themes of Advent.
Second	John the Baptist		
Third	John the Baptist		
Fourth	The events that prepared immediately for the birth of Jesus.	Readings from Isaiah have a special place in setting out this theme.	

The weekdays of Advent are divided into two parts: those before 17 December (general preparation) and those between 17 December and 24 December (immediate preparation). In each period, the themes of Sundays are extended and the focus is upon Isaiah, John the Baptist, and the opening chapters of Matthew's and Luke's gospels.[1]

But, we must repeat again: one can only appreciate these choices in the context of the overall liturgy of the particular day, and note how each day has a particular flavour depending on whether it is Year A, B, or C.

One final point: the feast of the Baptism of our Lord made its appearance in the calendar in the renewal after Vatican II. It is deliberately a feast that looks both ways: on the one hand it

---

1. For more detail, look at the *General Instruction on the Lectionary*, nn. 93-6.

forms an end to Christmastide (and has many of those themes at its core), but it is also the beginning of Ordinary Time. When we recognise that this feast does look back to Christmas and look forward to Ordinary Time, we appreciate it, and the Sundays of Ordinary Time, all the more.[2]

---

2. The rationale underlying particular choices of readings during Advent and Christmastide is examined in Thomas O'Loughlin, *Liturgical Resources for Advent and Christmastide* (Dublin: Columba, 2006).

CHAPTER FOUR

The Readings for Lent and Easter

Just as we have seen that the readings for Advent and Christmas are deliberately chosen to harmonise with the mystery / events being celebrated, so the same is true of our annual celebration of the Paschal Mystery at Easter, and the time of preparation for it: Lent. Moreover, there is also the special provision made for those communities who are welcoming new adult members using the *Rite of Christian Initiation of Adults* which affects the choices of readings for those communities. Because of these considerations, we can only give a few very broad overviews of the contents of the lectionary here.[1]

We shall look at this season under the following headings:
- Sundays of Lent
- Weekdays of Lent
- Easter Triduum
- Sundays of Eastertide
- Weekdays of Eastertide
- Ascension and Pentecost

Sundays of Lent
There are four guiding principles:

1. The gospel read on each Sunday is the key reading.

2. The Old Testament readings have been chosen to harmonise with the gospels.

3. The psalms have been chosen to provide a prayerful response to the Old Testament Readings.

---

1. For more detail, look at the *General Instruction on the Lectionary*, nn. 97-102.

4. The epistle readings have been chosen 'to fit the gospel and Old Testament readings and, to the extent possible, to provide a connection between them.'[2]

The gospel themes are:

Sunday	Year A (Mt)	Year B (Mk)	Year C (Lk)
	The accounts of the Lord's temptation and transfiguration are used on the first two Sundays.		
First	Mt 4:1-11	Mk 1:12-5	Lk 4:1-13
Second	Mt 17:1-9	Mk 9:2-10	Lk 9:28-36
Third	The Samaritan Woman: Jn 4:5-42	Jesus cleansing the temple: Jn 2:13-25	The call to repentance: Lk 13:1-9
Fourth	The man born blind: Jn 9:1-41	The Son of Man must be lifted up: Jn 3:14-21	Forgiveness as seen in the Prodigal Son parable: Lk 15:1-32
Fifth	The raising of Lazarus: Jn 11:1-45	The Son of Man is glorified: Jn 12:20-33	Forgiveness as seen in the incident of the woman caught in adultery: Jn 8:1-11
Palm	Matthew's passion narrative	Mark's passion narrative	Luke's passion narrative

---

2. *General Instruction on the Lectionary*, n. 97.

Weekdays of Lent
The gospels are chosen as relating to the season's themes.

The Old Testament readings are chosen as relating to the gospel.

The Easter Triduum (i.e. Holy Thursday Evening, Good Friday afternoon, the Easter Vigil)
All the readings are related to the events being celebrated as seen from the perspective of the church's memory of Jesus.

Sundays of Eastertide
All the readings are related in some way to the theme of the risen Christ who is now present in the community.

Gospels
On the first three Sundays the gospels 'recount the appearances of the risen Christ'.[3]

On the fourth Sunday, the theme of the Good Shepherd from John's gospel is read.

On the remaining Sundays, excerpts from 'the last supper discourse' in John are read.

Sunday	Year A	Year B	Year C
Easter day	Jn 20:1-9 – Easter morning		
Second	Jn 20:19-31 – the eighth day		
Third	Lk 24:13-35 – Emmaus	Lk 24:35-48 – 'Touch me and see'	Jn 21:1-19 – the wondrous haul of fish
Fourth	Jn 10:1-10	Jn 10:11-8	Jn 10:27-30
Fifth	Jn 14:1-12	Jn 15:1-8	Jn 13:31-5
Sixth	Jn 14:15-21	Jn 15:9-17	Jn 14:23-9
Seventh	Jn 17:1-11	Jn 17:11-9	Jn 17:20-6

3. *General Instruction on the Lectionary*, n. 100.

First Readings

These are taken from the Acts of the Apostles and over a three-year cycle are intended to show the life of the early churches.

Sunday	All references are to Acts		
	YEAR A	YEAR B	YEAR C
Easter day	10:34, 37-43		
Second	2:42-7	4:32-5	5:12-6
Third	2:14, 22-8	3:13-5, 17-9	5:27-32, 40-1
Fourth	2:14, 36-41	4:8-12	13:14, 43-52
Fifth	6:1-7	9:26-31	14:21-7
Sixth	8:5-8, 14-7	10:25-6, 34-5, 44-8	15:1-2, 22-9
Seventh	1:12-14	1:15-7, 20-6	7:55-60

This selection from Acts focuses on the church in Jerusalem in its earliest days. It is one of the weaknesses of the entire lectionary that the second half of Acts dealing with the travels of Paul and his churches around the rim of the Mediterranean is nowhere read in the regular cycles of readings.

These readings from Acts are not thematically linked to the gospels, except in that both relate to the earliest days of the church.

This is the only period in the year when the first readings on a Sunday are not from the Old Testament.

Second Readings (Epistles)

In Year A we read from 1 Peter, in Year B from 1 John (especially suitable as these are catecheses for young churches and they fit the mood of the liturgy in Eastertide), and in Year C we read from the Apocalypse which, while it does fit with the time, is not nearly so snug a fit as the readings for Years A and B.

These readings are not thematically linked to the gospels or first readings.

Weekdays of Eastertide

The weekday readings follow the same general pattern and further extend the exploration of the themes of the Sundays.

Ascension and Pentecost

The readings are focused on the events these feasts recall. All the readings are related to the theme of the day being celebrated.

Lastly, Eastertide is at the very heart of the Christian Year: to appreciate it fully, we have no better companion than the lectionary.[4]

---

4. The rationale underlying particular choices of readings during Lent and Eastertide is examined in Thomas O'Loughlin, *Liturgical Resources for Lent and Eastertide* (Dublin: Columba, 2004).

CHAPTER FIVE

The Sunday Readings for the Year of Matthew (A)

The fundamental lectionary dynamic in this year is the semi-continuous reading of Matthew (apart from the infancy narrative and the passion narrative), and each gospel reading determines its first reading from the Old Testament.

This chapter consists of:

- An overview of the sequence of gospel readings for this year with their accompanying first reading.
- A description of the larger 'lectionary units' into which the gospels on succeeding Sundays are seen to belong. These larger units are intended to help us see the overall perspective of each evangelist's preaching of the good news, his distinctive view of the Christ and his distinctive way of presenting him to the community who hears his gospel.
- A diagrammatic summary presentation of the lectionary units.
- An overview of the sequence of epistles (second readings) offered in the lectionary for this year.

The Sequence of Gospel Readings: An Overview
The purpose of this table is to show at a glance the sweep of readings through Matthew in Year A. We must remember, of course, that this sweep is always interrupted by Easter. It also shows at a glance that there is no sequence in the first readings, each being chosen as having some relationship with the gospel of the day.

Sunday	Gospel	First Reading
	Lectionary Unit I	
1 – Baptism	Mt 3:13-7	Isa 42:1-4, 6-7
2	Jn 1:29-34	Isa 49:3, 5-6
	Lectionary Unit II	
3	Mt 4:12-23	Isa 8:23 – 9:3
4	Mt 5:1-12	Zeph 2:3; 3:12-13
5	Mt 5:13-16	Isa 58:7-10
6	Mt 5:17-37	Sir 15:15-20
7	Mt 5:38-48	Lev 19:1-2, 17-18
8	Mt 6:24-34	Isa 49:14-15
9	Mt 7:21-27	Deut 11:18, 26-28, 32
	Lectionary Unit III	
10	Mt 9:9-13	Hos 6:3-6
11	Mt 9:36 – 10:8	Ex 19:2-6
12	Mt 10:26-33	Jer 20:10-13
13	Mt 10:37-42	2 Kgs 4:8-11, 14-16
	Lectionary Unit IV	
14	Mt 11:25-30	Zech 9:9-10
15	Mt 13:1-23	Isa 55:10-11
16	Mt 13:24-43	Wis 12:13, 16-19
17	Mt 13:44-52	1 Kgs 3:5, 7-12
	Lectionary Unit V	
18	Mt 14:13-21	Isa 55:1-3
19	Mt 14:22-33	1 Kgs 19:9, 11-13
20	Mt 15:21-28	Isa 56:1, 6-7
21	Mt 16:13-20	Isa 22:19-23
22	Mt 16:21-27	Jer 20:7-9
23	Mt 18:15-20	Ezek 33:7-9
24	Mt 18:21-35	Sir 27:30-28:7
	Lectionary Unit VI	
25	Mt 20:1-16	Isa 55:6-9
26	Mt 21:28-32	Ezek 18:25-28
27	Mt 21:33-43	Isa 5:1-7
28	Mt 22:1-14	Isa 25:6-10
29	Mt 22:15-21	Isa 45:1, 4-6

30	Mt 22:34-40	Ex 22:20-26
31	Mt 23:1-12	Mal 1:14-2:2, 8-10
32	Mt 25:1-13	Wis 6:12-16
33	Mt 25:14-30	Prov 31:10-31 (bits)
	Lectionary Unit VII	
34 – Christ the King	Mt 25:31-46	Ezek 34:11-12, 15-17

THE LECTIONARY UNITS

An Overarching Theme

The Year of Matthew is envisaged by the Lectionary as comprising seven units ranging in length from one Sunday (Unit VII) to
nine Sundays (Unit VI).

The core of the year is the five great 'sermons' that go to
make up Matthew's gospel, and these form Units II, III, IV, V,
and VI, preceded by Unit I on the figure of Jesus the Christ, and
concluded by the last Sunday of the year focusing on the fulfillment of God's kingdom (Unit VII).

In this year each Unit is made up of two types of text: some
narrative (over one or more Sundays), then some discourse (always over more than one Sunday).

The five sermons are:

The Sermon on the Mount (Sundays 4-9)

The Mission Sermon (Sundays 11-13)

The Parable Sermon (Sundays 15-17)

The Community Sermon (Sundays 23-24)

The Final Sermon (Sundays 32-33).

As with schematic divisions of the gospels, it is neater to look
at in the abstract than in terms of actual lections chosen.
However, it is worth bearing in mind the lectionary's desire to
respect, in so far as it can, the five-sermon structure of Matthew,
as it often helps us to appreciate the rationale behind making the
junctions occur where they do, and the choice of accompanying
first reading, which often functions as a lens highlighting a particular aspect of the gospel on a particular Sunday.

Lectionary Unit I

This consists of just two Sundays and focuses on The Figure of Jesus the Messiah.

The question, who is the Christ, is then explored with the story of Jesus's baptism (Sunday 1) and the witness of John the Baptist (Sunday 2).

Lectionary Unit II

This Unit comprises Sundays 3-9, and its focus is on Christ's design for life in God's kingdom.

There is one Sunday devoted to narrative: Sunday 3 which highlights the call of the first disciples.

The remaining Sundays' gospels are seen as discourse, which together make up the Sermon on the Mount.

Lectionary Unit III

This Unit comprises Sundays 10-13, and its focus is on the spread of God's kingdom.

There is one Sunday devoted to narrative: Sunday 10 which highlights the call of Levi.

The remaining Sundays' gospels are seen as discourse: the Mission Sermon.

Lectionary Unit IV

This Unit comprises Sundays 14-17, and its focus is on the mystery of God's kingdom.

There is one Sunday devoted to narrative: Sunday 13, whose theme is the revelation to the simple.

The remaining Sundays' gospels are seen as discourse, which together make up the Parable Sermon.

Lectionary Unit V

This Unit comprises Sundays 18-24, and its focus is on God's kingdom on earth – the church of Christ.

There are five Sundays devoted to narrative:

Sunday 18: the feeding of the five thousand;

Sunday 19: Jesus walking on water;

Sunday 20: the healing/exorcism of the Canaanite woman's daughter;

Sunday 21: Peter's confession of Jesus's identity (and to which the lectionary adds the comment 'the primacy conferred');

Sunday 22: discipleship and the prophecy of the passion.

This set of five Sundays has less unity than the other units in this year's lectionary, and the sequence of three Sundays each with a miracle story poses its own difficulties.

The remaining Sundays' gospels (Sundays 23 and 24) are seen as discourse: the Community Sermon.

Lectionary Unit VI

This Unit comprises Sundays 25-33, and the lectionary gives it the title of 'Authority and Invitation – the ministry ends.' However, it has far less unity of theme or focus than the other units.

Seven Sundays are presented as devoted to narrative: Sunday 25-31; then Sundays 32 and 33 are presented as discourse: the final sermon.

However, the narrative section begins with four Sundays on which parables are read (25-28), which are followed by three other elements which are located here as that is roughly where they fall in Matthew's gospel read continuously.

This unit's structure is an attempt to find a logic in Matthew's gospel, after the fact, and its rationale of 'narrative followed by discourse' is artificial.

Lectionary Unit VII

The Son of Man coming in glory is King

This unit consists of just one Sunday: Sunday 34, the Last Sunday of the Year, and the lectionary describes its focus as 'God's kingdom fulfilled'. The theme of the Sunday is the Matthaean presentation of Jesus as the king in judgement at the end of time.

In this Unit all three readings form a thematic unity; indeed in Year A the second reading and gospel supply, together, all the basic imagery that underpins the Feast of Christ the King

The units can be presented diagrammatically thus:

Year A: The Year of Matthew		
Unit	Type of Gospel	Sunday
1: The Figure of Jesus the Messiah		1
		2
2: Christ's design for life in God's kingdom	Narrative	3
		4
		5
	Discourse:	6
	The Sermon on the Mount	7
		8
		9
3: The Spread of God's Kingdom	Narrative	10
		11
	Discourse:	12
	The Mission Sermon	13
4: The Mystery of God's Kingdom	Narrative	14
		15
	Discourse:	16
	The Parable Sermon	17
5: God's Kingdom on Earth – The Church of Christ	Narrative	18
	Narrative	19
	Narrative	20
	Narrative	21
	Narrative	22
	Discourse:	23
	The Community Sermon	24

	Narrative	25
	Narrative	26
	Narrative	27
	Narrative	28
6: Authority and	Narrative	29
invitation –	Narrative	30
the ministry ends	Narrative	31
	Discourse:	32
	The Final Sermon	33
7: God's Kingdom fulfilled		34

THE SEQUENCE OF SECOND READINGS: AN OVERVIEW

The purpose of this table is to show at a glance the sweep of readings through the epistles in Year A. We must remember, of course, that this sweep is always interrupted by Easter.

Sunday	Reading
1 – Baptism	Acts 10:34-38
2	1 Cor 1:1-3
3	1 Cor 1:10-13, 17
4	1 Cor 1:26-31
5	1 Cor 2:1-5
6	1 Cor 2:6-10
7	1 Cor 3:16-23
8	1 Cor 4:1-5
9	Rom 3:21-25, 28
10	Rom 4:18-25
11	Rom 5:6-11
12	Rom 5:12-15
13	Rom 6:3-4, 8-11
14	Rom 8:9, 11-13
15	Rom 8:18-23
16	Rom 8:26-27
17	Rom 8:28-30
18	Rom 8:35, 37-39

19	Rom 9:1-5
20	Rom 11:13-15, 29-32
21	Rom 11:33-36
22	Rom 12:1-2
23	Rom 13:8-10
24	Rom 14:7-9
25	Phil 1:20-24, 27
26	Phil 2:1-11
27	Phil 4:6-9
28	Phil 4:12-14, 19-20
29	1 Thess 1:1-5
30	1 Thess 1:5-10
31	1 Thess 2:7-9, 13
32	1 Thess 4:13-18
33	1 Thess 5:1-6
34 – Christ the King	1 Cor 15:20-26, 28

CHAPTER 6

The Sunday Readings for the Year of Mark (B)

The fundamental lectionary dynamic in this year is the semi-continuous reading of Mark (apart from the passion narrative), along with some passages from John, and each gospel reading determines its first reading from the Old Testament.

This chapter consists of:

- An overview of the sequence of gospel readings for this year with their accompanying first reading.
- A description of the larger 'lectionary units' into which the gospels on succeeding Sundays are seen to belong. These larger units are intended to help us see the overall perspective of each evangelist's preaching of the good news, and his distinctive view of the Christ and his distinctive way of presenting him to the community who hears his gospel.
- A diagrammatic summary presentation of the lectionary units.
- An overview of the sequence of epistles (second readings) offering in the lectionary for this year.

THE SEQUENCE OF GOSPEL READINGS: AN OVERVIEW

The purpose of this table is to show at a glance the sweep of readings through Mark and John in Year B. We must remember, of course, that this sweep is always interrupted by Easter. It also shows at a glance that there is no sequence in the first readings, each being chosen as having some relationship with the gospel of the day.

Sunday	Gospel	First Reading
	Lectionary Unit I	
1 – Baptism	Mk 1:6b-11	Isa 55:1-11
2	Jn 1:35-42	1 Sam 3:3-10, 19
	Lectionary Unit II – Stage I	
3	Mk 1:14-20	Jon 3:1-5, 10
4	Mk 1:21-8	Dt 18:15-20
5	Mk 1:29-39	Job 7:1-4, 6-7
6	Mk 1:40-5	Lev 13:1-2, 45-6
7	Mk 2:1-12	Isa 43:18-9, 21-2, 24-5
8	Mk 2:18-22	Hos 2:16-7, 21-2
9	Mk 2:23–3:6	Dt 5:12-15
	Lectionary Unit II – Stage II	
10	Mk 3:20-35	Gn 3:9-15
11	Mk 4:26-34	Ezek 17:22-4
12	Mk 4:35-41	Job 38:1, 8-11
13	Mk 5:21-43	Wis 1:13-5; 2:23-4
14	Mk 6:1-6	Ezek 2:2-5
	Lectionary Unit II – Stage III	
15	Mk 6:7-13	Amos 7:12-5
16	Mk 6:30-4	Jer 23:1-6
17	Jn 6:1-15	2 Kgs 4:42-4
18	Jn 6:24-35	Ex 16:2-4, 12-5
19	Jn 6:41-52	1 Kgs 19:4-8
20	Jn 6:51-58	Prov 9:1-6
21	Jn 6:61-70	Jos 24:1-2, 15-8
22	Mk 7:1-8, 14-5, 21	Dt 4:1-2, 6-8
23	Mk 7:31-7	Isa 35:4-7
	Lectionary Unit III – Stage I	
24	Mk 8:27-35	Isa 50:5-9
25	Mk 9:29-36	Wis 2:12, 17-20
26	Mk 9:37-42, 44,46-7	Nm 11:25-9
27	Mk 10:2-16	Gn 2:18-24
28	Mk 10:17-30	Wis 7:7-11
29	Mk 10:35-45	Isa 53:10-11
30	Mk 10:46-52	Jer 31:7-9

Lectionary Unit III – Stage II

31	Mk 12:28b-34	Dt 6:2-6
32	Mk 12:38-44	1 Kgs 17:10-16
33	Mk 13:24-32	Dan 12:1-3

Lectionary Unit III – Stage III

34 – Christ the King	Jn 18:33b-37	Dan 7:13-4

THE LECTIONARY UNITS

Lectionary Unity I

This unit consists of just two Sundays which are seen to open the year/the gospel by focusing on the figure of Jesus the Messiah. This is expressed on the Feast of the Baptism (Sunday 1) with Mark's account, and then the call of Andrew and his companion from John's gospel (Sunday 2). The two events taken together provide the witness from heaven and earth to Jesus being the Promised One.

Lectionary Unit II.I

This unit consists of twenty one Sundays (Sundays 3 to 23 inclusive) whose overall theme is the Mystery of Jesus being progressively revealed. It is made up of three stages:

I.   Jesus with the Jewish crowds.
II.   Jesus with his disciples.
III.   Jesus's manifestation of himself.

The first stage runs from the third to the ninth Sunday. In these gospels we encounter Jesus around the Sea of Galilee, healing a leper and a paralytic, and answering questions about fasting and the Sabbath.

Lectionary Unity II.II

The second stage of this unit, which is concerned with the Mystery of Jesus being progressively revealed, focuses on Jesus with his disciples.

This stage runs from the tenth to the fourteenth Sunday. In these gospels we encounter Jesus facing serious criticism, preaching parables of the kingdom, calming the storm, healing, and being rejected at Nazareth.

Lectionary Unity II.III

This stage of the second unit (whose overall theme is the Mystery of Jesus being progressively revealed) focuses on Jesus's manifestation of himself.

This stage is unusual in the lectionary for Ordinary Time in that it is made up of sections from John as well as Mark. It begins with two Sundays (15-16) where Jesus gives The Twelve their mission and then manifests compassion on the crowds. This mention of crowds around Jesus is then the cue for a five-Sunday selection from Jn 6 on the Eucharist. The stage then concludes with two more gospel readings from Mark on Sundays 22 and 23.

Lectionary Unit III.I

This unit consists of eleven Sundays (Sundays 24 to 34 inclusive) whose overall theme is the Mystery of the Son of Man. It is made up of three units:

    I.   The 'Way' of the Son of Man.
    II.   The final revelation in Jerusalem.
    III. The fulfillment of the mystery.

The first stage runs from the twenty-fourth to the thirtieth Sunday. It opens with Peter's confession of faith and then the narrative that immediately follows in Mark.

Lectionary Unit III.II

This stage consists of three Sundays (Sundays 31 to 33 inclusive) when we read of the final revelation of the identity of the Son of Man in Jerusalem.

Lectionary Unit III.III

This stage consists of the last Sunday of Ordinary Time, when the Feast of Christ the King is seen as the liturgical celebration of the fulfillment of the mystery of the Son of Man.

Although this is seen as the culmination of the Year of Mark, the end of the year's reflection on the Eschaton is taken from John.

The units can be presented diagrammatically thus:

Year B: The Year of Mark		
Unit	**Stage**	**Sunday**
1: The Figure of Jesus the Messiah		1 2
2. The Mystery progressively revealed	1. Jesus with the Jewish Crowds	3 4 5 6 7 8 9
	2. Jesus with his disciples	10 11 12 13 14 15 16 17
	3. Jesus manifests himself	18 19 20 21 22 23

		24
		25
	1.	26
	The 'Way'	27
3.	of the Son of Man	28
The Mystery		29
of the Son of Man		30
	2.	31
	Final revelation	32
	in Jerusalem	33
	3.	34
	The fulfillment of the mystery	

THE SEQUENCE OF SECOND READINGS: AN OVERVIEW

The purpose of this table is to show at a glance the sweep of readings through the epistles in Year B. We must remember, of course, that this sweep is always interrupted by Easter.

Sunday	Reading
1 – Baptism	1 Jn 5:1-9
2	1 Cor 6:13-15, 17-20
3	1 Cor 7:29-31
4	1 Cor 7:32-35
5	1 Cor 9:16-9, 22-3
6	1 Cor 10:31-11:1
7	2 Cor 1:18-22
8	2 Cor 3:1-6
9	2 Cor 4:6-11
10	2 Cor 4:13-5:1
11	2 Cor 5:6-10
12	2 Cor 5:14-17
13	2 Cor 8:7, 9, 13-5
14	2 Cor 12:7-10
15	Eph 1:3-14
16	Eph 2:13-8

17	Eph 4:1-6
18	Eph 4:17, 20-4
19	Eph 4:30-5:2
20	Eph 5:15-20
21	Eph 5:21-32
22	Jas 1:17-8, 21-2, 27
23	Jas 2:1-5
24	Jas 2:14-8
25	Jas 3:16-4:3
26	Jas 5:1-6
27	Heb 2:9-11
28	Heb 4:12-3
29	Heb 4:14-6
30	Heb 5:1-6
31	Heb 7:23-8
32	Heb 9:24-8
33	Heb 10:11-4, 18
34 – Christ the King	Apoc 1:5-8

CHAPTER 7

The Sunday Readings for the Year of Luke (C)

The fundamental lectionary dynamic in this year is the semi-continuous reading of Luke (apart from the infancy narrative and the passion narrative), and each gospel reading determines its first reading from the Old Testament.

This chapter consists of:

- An overview of the sequence of gospel readings for this year with their accompanying first reading.
- A description of the larger 'lectionary units' into which the gospels on succeeding Sundays are seen to belong. These larger units are intended to help us see the overall perspective of each evangelist's preaching of the good news, and his distinctive view of the Christ and his distinctive way of presenting him to the community who hears his gospel.
- A diagrammatic summary presentation of the lectionary units.
- An overview of the sequence of epistles (second readings) offering in the lectionary for this year.

THE SEQUENCE OF GOSPEL READINGS: AN OVERVIEW

The purpose of this table is to show at a glance the sweep of readings through Luke in Year C. We must remember, of course, that this sweep is always interrupted by Easter. It also shows at a glance that there is no sequence in the first readings, each being chosen as having some relationship with the gospel of the day.

Sunday	Gospel	First Reading
	Lectionary Unit I	
1 – Baptism	Lk 3:15-6; 21-2	Isa 40:1-5; 9-11
2	Jn 2:1-12	Isa 62:1-5
	Lectionary Unit II	
3	Lk 1:1-4; 4:14-21	Neh 8:2-6; 8-10
4	Lk 4:21-30	Jer 1:4-5; 17-9
	Lectionary Unit III	
5	Lk 5:1-11	Isa 6:1-8
6	Lk 6:17; 20-26	Jer 17:5-8
7	Lk 6:27-38	1 Sam 26:2;7-9; 12-13; 22-23
8	Lk 6:39-45	Sir 27:4-7
9	Lk 7:1-10	1 Kgs 8:41-3
10	Lk 7:11-7	1 Kgs 17:17-24
11	Lk 7:36-8:3	2 Sam 12:7-10; 13
12	Lk 9: 18-24	Zech 12:10-11
	Lectionary Unit IV	
13	Lk 9:51-62	1 Kgs 19:16; 19-21
14	Lk 10:1-12; 17-20	Isa 66:10-14
15	Lk 10:25-37	Dt 30:10-14
16	Lk 10:38-42	Gen 18:1-10
17	Lk 11:1-13	Gen 18:20-32
18	Lk 12:13-21	Qo 1:2; 2:21-3
19	Lk 12: 32-48	Wis 18:6-9
20	Lk 12:49-53	Jer 38:4-6; 8-10
21	Lk 13:22-30	Isa 66:18-21
22	Lk 14:1; 7-14	Sir 3:17-20; 28-9
23	Lk 14: 25-33	Wis 9:13-8
	Lectionary Unit V	
24	Lk 15:1-32	Ex 32:7-11; 13-4
	Lectionary Unit VI	
25	Lk 16:1-13	Amos 8:4-7
26	Lk 16:19-31	Amos 6:1; 4-7
27	Lk 17:5-10	Hab 1:2-3; 2:2-4
28	Lk 17:11-19	2 Kgs 5:14-7

29	Lk 18:1-8	Ex 17:8-13
30	Lk 18:9-14	Sir 35:12-4; 16-9
31	Lk 19:1-10	Wis 11:22-12:2
	Lectionary Unit VII	
32	Lk 20:27-38	Macc 7:1-2; 9-14
33	Lk 21:5-19	Mal 3:19-20
	Lectionary Unit VIII	
34 – Christ the King	Lk 23:35-43	2 Sam 5:1-3

THE LECTIONARY UNITS

An Overarching Theme

The Year of Luke is envisaged by the Lectionary as comprising eight units ranging in length from one Sunday (Units V and VIII) to eleven Sundays (Unit IV).

We can see Luke's agenda as broadly geographical and spread over his two works: the gospel and Acts.

Jesus travels from

Nazareth to Jerusalem and death and resurrection and his return to the Father.

The church travels from

Jerusalem to the Earth's Ends through suffering and death to glory.

The Lectionary consciously adopts this theme, and Luke's travel narrative (chapters 9-19) provides the readings for the core of Ordinary Time: Sundays 13-31. This journey is more chronological in structure than geographical, and so is well suited to being read sequentially in time, Sunday after Sunday.

This journey is also assumed to parallel the journey of the People of God, both collectively and as individuals for it is the journey through life's sufferings and joys. The Lectionary expects that each Sunday be seen in the light of the larger units (groups of Sundays) and the whole journey theme.

Lectionary Unit I

This consists of just two Sundays and focuses on The Figure of Jesus the Messiah.

The question, who is the Christ, is then explored with the story of Jesus's baptism (Sunday 1) and the manifestation of his glory at the wedding in Cana (Sunday 2).

Lectionary Unit II
Luke's Programme

The second unit is made up of two Sundays with a common theme – indeed they share a single narrative section of the gospel – which is Luke's programme for the ministry of Jesus.

It consists of Sundays 3 and 4 both of which focus on Jesus's visit to the synagogue in Nazareth. These two Sundays (with the prologue and Jesus's identification of himself as the one fulfilling the prophecy of Isaiah) set the tone for the year: the Jubilee Year has come and with it a new relationship of righteousness between God and his people and so a new relationship of justice among God's people is called for.

Lectionary Unit III
Galilee

This unit is devoted to Jesus's ministry in Galilee. It runs from Sunday 5 to Sunday 12, and contains seven or eight Sundays depending on whether a particular year has thirty-three or thirty-four Sundays in total. This is probably the least useful unit from the standpoint of preaching or teaching as it is always broken up by the period of Lent-Eastertide-Trinity (and in some places Corpus Christi).

Its sections / themes are:

Sunday 5	*The call of the first apostles*
Sunday 6	The sermon on the plain (1)
Sunday 7	The sermon on the plain (2)
Sunday 8	The sermon on the plain (3)
Sunday 9	Curing the centurion's servant
Sunday 10	*The widow at Naim/Nain*

Sunday 11   *The woman anoints Jesus's feet*
Sunday 12   Peter's confession of faith

The sections of the gospel referred to in italics above are incidents that are only found in Luke's gospel and so are texts that are only preached upon on these Sundays in the Three-Year Cycle, whereas the Lukan texts on the other Sundays may be verbally very similar to texts met elsewhere in the gospels and consequently read on other Sundays over the three years.

Lectionary Unit IV
Towards Jerusalem
This unit is devoted to the first part of the 'Travel Narrative' and its theme is the qualities Jesus demands of those who follow him.

It runs from Sunday 13 to Sunday 23, and contains eleven Sundays. Its sections / themes are:

Sunday 13   *The journey begins*
Sunday 14   *The mission of the seventy-two*
Sunday 15   *The Good Samaritan*
Sunday 16   *At the meal in the house of Martha and Mary*
Sunday 17   *The friend in need*
Sunday 18   *The parable of the rich fool building barns*
Sunday 19   The need for vigilance
Sunday 20   Jesus brings 'not peace but division'
Sunday 21   Few will be saved
Sunday 22   True humility
Sunday 23   The cost of discipleship

The sections of the gospel referred to in italics above are incidents that are only found in Luke's gospel and so are texts that are only preached upon on those Sundays in the Three-Year Cycle, whereas Luke's text on the other Sundays may be verbally very similar to texts met elsewhere in the gospels and consequently read on other Sundays over the three years.

Lectionary Unit V
Pardon and Reconciliation
This unit consists of just one Sunday: Sunday 24. Its focus is on the 'gospel within the gospel': Jesus's message of pardon and reconciliation. It is devoted to Lk 15 (all but three verses of which are only found in this gospel) and which consists of a string of three parables: (1) the lost coin, (2) the lost sheep, and (3) the prodigal son.

Lectionary Unit VI
Towards Jerusalem, again
This unit is devoted to the second part of the 'travel narrative' and explores the obstacles facing those who follow Jesus.

It runs from Sunday 25 to Sunday 31. Its sections/themes are:

Sunday 25   *The unjust steward*
Sunday 26   *The rich man and Lazarus*
Sunday 27   *A lesson on faith and dedication*
Sunday 28   *The ten lepers*
Sunday 29   *The unjust judge*
Sunday 30   *The Pharisee and the Tax-collector*
Sunday 31   *Meeting Zacchaeus*

In many ways this is the most characteristic section of Luke's gospel for none of these sections, stories, incidents are found elsewhere in the gospels.

Lectionary Unit VII
In Jerusalem
This unit is devoted to Jesus's ministry in Jerusalem. It consists of just Sunday 32 and Sunday 33, and it has an eschatological theme running through it.

On Sunday 32 we have the debate about the nature of the resurrection, and then on Sunday 33 we have 'the signs' announcing the End.

Lectionary Unit VIII
The Christ is King
This unit consists of just one Sunday: Sunday 34, the Last Sunday of the Year.

The focus is upon reconciliation and this is expressed through reading the account of the repentant thief from the passion narrative. This story is only found in Luke's gospel.

The units can be presented diagrammatically thus:

Year C: The Year of Luke		
Unit	Note	Sunday
1: The Figure of Jesus		1
the Messiah		2
2: Luke's programme		3
for Jesus's ministry		4
		5
		6
		7
		8
3: The Galilean Ministry		9
	found only in Luke	10
	found only in Luke	11
		12
	found only in Luke	13
	found only in Luke	14
4: The first part of the	*found only in Luke*	15
'travel narrative'	*found only in Luke*	16
–	*found only in Luke*	17
	found only in Luke	18
		19
qualities Jesus demands		20
in his followers		21
		22
		23

5: The 'gospel within the gospel': Pardon and Reconciliation	*found only in Luke*	24
	found only in Luke	25
6: The second part of the	*found only in Luke*	26
'travel narrative'	*found only in Luke*	27
–	*found only in Luke*	28
the obstacles facing those	*found only in Luke*	29
who follow Jesus	*found only in Luke*	30
	found only in Luke	31
7: The ministry in		32
Jerusalem		33
8: Christ the King: Reconciliation	*found only in Luke*	34

THE SEQUENCE OF SECOND READINGS: AN OVERVIEW

The purpose of this table is to show at a glance the sweep of readings through the epistles in Year C. We must remember, of course, that this sweep is always interrupted by Easter.

Sunday	Reading
1 – Baptism	Tit 2:11-4; 3:4-7
2	1 Cor 12:4-11
3	1 Cor 12:12-30
4	1 Cor 12: 31-13:13
5	1 Cor 15:1-11
6	1 Cor 15:12; 16-20
7	1 Cor 15:45-49
8	1 Cor 15:54-8
9	Gal 1:1-2; 6-10
10	Gal 1:11-9
11	Gal 2:16; 19-21
12	Gal 3:26-9
13	Gal 5:1; 13-8
14	Gal 6:14-8

15	Col 1:15-20
16	Col 1:24-8
17	Col 2:12-4
18	Col 3:1-5; 9-11
19	Heb 11:1-2; 8-19
20	Heb 12:1-4
21	Heb 12:5-7; 11-3
22	Heb 12:18-9; 22-4
23	Philemon 9-10; 12-17
24	1 Tim 1:12-7
25	1 Tim 2:1-8
26	1 Tim 6:11-6
27	2 Tim 1:6-8; 13-4
28	2 Tim 2:8-13
29	2 Tim 3:14-4:2
30	2 Tim 4:6-8; 16-8
31	2 Thess 1:11-2:2
32	2 Thess 2:16-3:5
33	2 Thess 3:7-12
34 – Christ the King	Col 1:11-20

CHAPTER EIGHT

The Weekday Readings for Ordinary Time

When we think of readings at the Eucharist, we think immediately of the community's celebration on Sundays – and this is appropriate as the Sunday gathering is *the* gathering of Christians and has been since before we even had written gospels. However, the Eucharist is celebrated on weekdays as well with smaller gatherings and there is a carefully planned lectionary – distinct from the Sunday plans – for these days also. We have already looked at weekdays for the two special seasons in the chapters on Advent/Christmas and Lent/Easter, now it is time to look at the weekdays of Ordinary Time.

This chapter will look at three topics:

• The overall structure and plan of this lectionary
• The content of this lectionary
• The pastoral purpose of this lectionary

I STRUCTURE

The Lectionary for weekdays in Ordinary Time was compiled to stand-alone: firstly, it has a completeness and integrity of its own; secondly, it is independent of both the seasons and of the Sunday Lectionary for Ordinary Time. The fundamental driving force behind it was that it should lay out in an orderly way an experience of the whole scriptural memory of the church for people who would have time to reflect on this day after day. So one of its assumptions is that those who take part in the Eucharist on weekdays probably do so on a regular basis (e.g. the group of people who are the 'regular' weekday group at the Eucharist in any parish or people in religious orders who gather for the Eucharist daily). Such people would have, over the course of a two year period, virtually the whole panoply of Scripture offered to them at the Table of the Word. In short, anyone who attends the Eucharist regularly over two years should encounter virtually every book in both Old and New Testaments, hear of the great narratives that have formed our memory as a community, and have a feeling for the enormous variety of kinds of writing (e.g. theological myth in Genesis; proverbial wisdom in Sirach; remembered history in 1 Samuel; prophesy in Jeremiah; letters in Paul; visions in Apocalypse, and on and on) that have been included in the Scriptures.

To achieve this it did the following:

1. Since the primary reason for our gathering is to become the Body of Christ, the gospel is a focal point. The three synoptics are read each year (without their passion/resurrection narratives which are read in Eastertide, and in the case of Matthew and Luke without their infancy gospels which are read at Christmas). So, each year, the core 'ordinary parts' of the gospels – what Jesus did and said while among us in the flesh – form our memory in Ordinary Time. This cycle of gospels is annual, and this means that anyone who participates daily in the Eucharist should have heard three gospels in their entirety over the course of a year.

2. To present a sweep through the rest of our scriptural memory it has a two-year cycle of first readings which present each year a selection of passages from the books of each testament. These readings have no automatic or thematic link with the gospels that occur on the same day.

3. We have to think of the three cycles (gospels, first reading in Year 1, and first reading in Year 2) as wholly separate from each other. All three work on the principle of semi-continuous reading. This means that some books are covered in quite some detail (e.g. all the famous stories in Genesis in Year 1) but others get just a mention (e.g. Malachi in Year 1, Week 27). This reminds us that the books in the Scriptures are valued by us as parts of our memory – and not all memories are of equal importance – and not as religious communications from God which are

intrinsically valuable as such. The Lord becomes known to us in
his living Word, not in the pages of an ancient text – its task is to
spark our memory and imagination.

4. The psalms each day are linked to the first reading and intended to be a meditation upon them. A good example to examine is Year 1, Week 6, Thursday to see how the relationship
should work.

5. The gospel acclamations ('Alleluias') come from a common
pool (Lectionary, vol II, pp 901-7) and so those printed for each
day can be changed. These are intended to link forward to the
gospel: it is a preparation for the gospel, not a conclusion to the
psalm. Unfortunately, in many places, this has become the tail-
end of the reader's bit, and so seems to be the end of the psalm,
before she/he hands over to the deacon/priest for the gospel.
When such an impression is given, a part of the logic of the lectionary is destroyed.

6. Given that these readings are chosen by cycles of semi-continuous reading, we should not expect them to link with the
time of year – and generally they do not. The exception is in the
last weeks of Ordinary Time when in Year 1 Daniel is read,
while in Year 2 the Apocalypse is read. This is the only exposure
in the cycles to the apocalyptic literature and it fits with the
overall eschatological tone of these weeks set on the Sundays.

7. Year 1 is read in years whose dates are odd numbers (e.g.
1997, 2001, 2011); Year 2 is read in the other years (e.g. 1998,
2002, 2012).

8. These readings are intended to have priority – because the
whole aim of the lectionary for Ordinary Time is to present a
wide semi-continuous sweep of readings – over saints' days,
themed celebrations of the Eucharist, and pet choices for groups
or celebrants. Every time these cycles are interrupted the whole
communication value of the lectionary in forming the memory
of the community of the church is damaged.

9. These cycles for Ordinary Time are always interrupted by
Lent-Easter.

II CONTENT

There are 34 weeks in Ordinary Time, and six weekdays, which gives us a lectionary covering 204 days of the year. Moreover, there is a two-year cycle for the first reading on these days which means we have 408 combinations of readings provided in the lectionary.

The annual cycle of gospel readings (semi-continuous reading of Mark, Matthew, and Luke – less their infancy and passion narratives) can be seen by looking the gospel column of this table. The first readings (two sweeps through the Old and New Testament books spread over a two-year cycle) are distinct from the gospels and each year's selection should be seen as an independent set of readings designed to give a broad taste each year of the two Testaments.

	Gospel	Year 1	Year 2
Week 1			
	Mark	**Hebrews**	**1 Samuel**
Mon	1:14-20	1:1-6	1:1-8
Tues	1:21-8	2:5-12	1:9-20
Wed	1:29-39	2:14-8	3:1-10, 19-20
Thur	1:40-5	3:7-14	4:1-11
Fri	2:1-12	4:1-5, 11	8:4-7, 10-22
Sat	2:13-7	4:12-6	9:1-4, 17-9, 10:1
Week 2			
Mon	2:18-22	5:1-10	15:16-23
Tues	2:23-8	6:10-20	16:1-13
Wed	3:1-6	7:1-3, 15-7	17:32-3, 37, 40-51
Thur	3:7-12	7:25-8:6	18:6-9; 19:1-7
Fri	3:13-9	8:6-13	24:3-21
			2 Samuel
Sat	3:20-1	9:2-3, 11-4	1:1-4, 11-2, 17, 19, 23-7
Week 3			
Mon	3:22-30	9:15, 24-8	5:1-7, 10
Tues	3:31-5	10:1-10	6:12-5, 17-9

Wed	4:1-20	10:11-8	7:4-17
Thur	4:21-5	10:19-25	7:18-9, 24-9
Fri	4:26-34	10:32-9	11:1-10, 13-7
Sat	4:35-41	11:1-2, 8-9	12:1-7, 10-7
Week 4			
Mon	5:1-20	11:32-40	15:13-4, 30; 16:5-13
Tues	5:21-43	12:1-4	18:9-10, 14, 24-5, 30-19:3
Wed	6:1-6	12:4-7, 11-5	24:2, 9-17
			1 Kings
Thur	6:7-13	12:18-9, 21-4	2:1-4, 10-2
			Sirach *(Ecclesiasticus)*
Fri	6:14-29	13:1-8	47:2-11
			1 Kings
Sat	6:30-4	13:15-7, 20-1	3:4-13
Week 5			
		Genesis 1-11	
Mon	6:53-6	1:1-19	8:1-7, 9-13
Tues	7:1-13	1:20-2:4	8:22-3, 27-30
Wed	7:14-23	2:4-9, 15-7	10:1-10
Thur	7:24-30	2:18-25	11:4-13
Fri	7:31-7	3:1-8	11:29-32; 12:19
Sat	8:1-10	3:9-24	12:26-32; 13:33-4
Week 6			
			James
Mon	8:11-3	4:1-15, 25	1:1-11
Tues	8:14-21	6:5-8; 7:1-5, 10	1:12-8
Wed	8:22-6	8:6-13, 20-2	1:19-27
Thur	8:27-33	9:1-13	2:1-9
Fri	8:34-9:1	11:1-9	2:14-24, 26
Sat	9:2-13	**Heb** 11:1-7	3:1-10

Week 7

		Sirach *(Ecclesiasticus)*	
Mon	9:14-29	1:1-10	3:13-8
Tues	9:30-7	2:1-11	4:1-10
Wed	9:38-40	4:11-9	4:13-7
Thur	9:41-50	5:1-8	5:1-6
Fri	10:1-12	6:5-17	5:9-12
Sat	10:13-6	17:1-15	5:13-20

Week 8

			1 Peter
Mon	10:17-27	17:24-9	1:3-9
Tues	10:28-31	35:1-12	1:10-6
Wed	10:32-45	36:1, 4-5, 10-7	1:18-25
Thur	10:46-52	42:15-25	2:2-5, 9-12
Fri	11:11-26	44:1, 9-13	4:7-13
			Jude
Sat	11:27-33	51:12-20	17, 20-5

Week 9

		Tobit	**2 Peter**
Mon	12:1-12	1:3; 2:1-8	1:2-7
Tues	12:13-7	2:9-14	3:11-5, 17-8
			2 Timothy
Wed	12:18-27	3:1-11, 16-7	1:1-3, 6-12
Thur	12:28-34	6:10-1; 7:1, 9-14; 8:4-9	2:8-15
Fri	12:35-7	11:5-17	3:10-7
Sat	12:38-44	12:1, 5-15, 20	4:1-8

Week 10

	Matthew	**2 Cor**	**1 Kings**
Mon	5:1-12	1:1-7	17:1-6
Tues	5:13-6	1:18-22	17:7-16
Wed	5:17-9	3:4-11	18:20-39
Thur	5:20-6	3:15-4:1, 3-6	18:41-6
Fri	5:27-32	4:7-15	19:9, 11-6
Sat	5:33-7	5:14-21	19:19-21

Week 11

Mon	5:38-42	6:1-10	21:1-16
Tues	5:43-8	8:1-9	21:17-29
			2 Kings
Wed	6:1-6, 16-8	9:6-11	2:1, 6-14
			Sirach
			(Ecclesiasticus)
Thur	6:7-15	11:1-11	48:1-14
			2 Kings
Fri	6:19-23	11:18, 21-30	11:1-4, 9-18, 20
			2 Chronicles
Sat	6:24-34	12:1-10	24:17-25

Week 12

		Gen 12-50	**2 Kings**
Mon	7:1-5	12:1-9	17:5-8, 13-5, 18
Tues	7:26, 12-4	13:2, 5-18	19:9-11, 14-21, 31-6
Wed	7:15-20	15:1-12, 17-8	22:8-13; 23; 1-3
Thur	7:21-9	16:1-12, 15-6	24:8-17
Fri	8:1-4	17:1, 9-10, 15-20	25:1-12
			Lamentations
Sat	8:5-17	18:1-15	2:2, 10-4, 18-9

Week 13

			Amos
Mon	8:18-22	18:16-33	2:6-10, 13-6
Tues	8:23-7	19:15-29	3:1-8; 4:11-2
Wed	8:28-34	21:5, 8-20	5:14-5, 21-4
Thur	9:1-8	22:1-19	7:10-7
Fri	9:9-13	23:>1-4, 19; 24:1-8, 62-7	8:4-6, 9-12
Sat	9:14-17	27:1-5, 15-29	9:11-5

Week 14

			Hosea
Mon	9:18-26	28:10-22	2:16-8, 21-2
Tues	9:32-8	32:23-33	8:4-7, 11-3

Wed	10:1-7	41:55-7; 42:5-7, 17-24	10:1-3, 7-8, 12
Thur	10:7-15	44:18-21, 23-9; 44:1-5	11:1, 3-4, 8-9
Fri	10:16-23	46:1-7, 28-30	14:2-10
			Isaiah
Sat	10:24-38	49:29-33; 50:15-26	6:1-8
Week 15			
		Exodus	
Mon	10:34-11:1	1:8-14, 22	1:11-7
Tues	11:20-4	2:1-15	7:1-9
Wed	11:25-7	3:1-6, 9-12	10:5-7, 13-6
Thur	11:28-30	3:13-20	26:7-9, 12, 16-9
Fri	12:1-8	11:10-12:14	38:1-6, 21-2, 7-8
			Micah
Sat	12:14-21	12:37-42	2:1-5
Week 16			
Mon	12:38-42	14:5-18	6:1-4, 6-8
Tues	12:46-50	14:21-15:1	7:14-5, 18-20
			Jeremiah
Wed	13:1-9	16:1-5, 9-15	1:1, 4-10
Thur	13:10-7	19:1-2, 9-11, 16-20	2:1-3, 7-8, 12-3
Fri	13:18-23	20:1-17	3:14-7
Sat	13:24-30	24:3-8	7:1-11
Week 17			
Mon	13:31-5	32:15-24, 30-4	13:1-11
Tues	13:36-43	33:7-11; 34:5-9, 28	14:17-22
Wed	13:44-6	34:29-35	15:10, 16-21
Thur	13:47-53	40:16-21, 34-8	18:1-6
		Leviticus	
Fri	13:54-8	23:1, 4-11, 15-6, 27, 34-7	26:1-9
Sat	14:1-12	25:1, 8-17	26:11-6, 24

Week 18

		Numbers	
Mon	14:13-21 (Years B and C); 14:22-36 (Year A)	11:4-15	28:1-17
Tues	14:22-36 (Years B and C); 15:1-2, 10-4 (Year A)	12:1-13	30:1-2, 12-5, 18-22
Wed	15:21-8	13:1-2, 25-14:1, 26-9, 34-5	31:1-7
Thur	16:13-23	20:1-13	31:31-4
		Deut	**Nahum**
Fri	16:24-8	4:32-40	2:1, 3; 3:1-3, 6-7
			Habakkuk
Sat	17:14-20	6:4-13	1:12-2:4

Week 19

			Ezekiel
Mon	17:22-7	10:12-22	1:2-5, 24-8
Tues	18:1-5, 10, 12-4	31:1-8	2:8-3:4
Wed	18:15-20	34:1-12	9:1-7; 10:18-22
		Joshua	
Thur	18:21-19:1	3:7-11, 13-7	12:1-12
Fri	19:3-12	24:1-13	16:1-15, 60, 63 *or* 16:59-63
Sat	19:13-5	24:14-29	18:1-10, 13, 30-2

Week 20

		Judges	
Mon	19:16-22	2:11-9	24:15-24
Tues	19:23-30	6:11-24	28:1-10
Wed	20:1-16	9:6-15	34:1-11
Thur	22:1-14	11:29-39	36:23-8
		Ruth	
Fri	22:34-40	1:1, 3-6, 14-6, 22	37:1-4

Sat	23:1-12	2:1-3, 8-11; 4:13-7	43:1-7

Week 21

		1 Thess	2 Thess
Mon	23:13-22	1:1-5, 8-10	1:1-5, 11-2
Tues	23:23-6	2:1-8	2:1-3, 14-7
Wed	23:27-32	2:9-13	3:6-10, 16-8
			1 Cor
Thur	24:42-51	3:7-13	1:1-9
Fri	25:1-13	4:1-8	1:17-25
Sat	25:14-30	4:9-11	1:26-31

Week 22

	Luke		
Mon	4:16-30	4:13-8	2:1-5
Tues	4:31-7	5:1-6, 9-11	2:10-6
		Colossians	
Wed	4:38-44	1:1-8	3:1-9
Thur	5:1-11	1:9-14	3:18-23
Fri	5:33-9	1:15-20	4:1-5
Sat	6:1-5	1:21-3	4:6-15

Week 23

Mon	6:6-11	1:24-2:3	5:1-8
Tues	6:12-9	2:6-15	6:1-11
Wed	6:20-6	3:1-11	7:25-31
Thur	6:27-38	3:12-7	8:1-7, 11-3
		1 Timothy	
Fri	6:39-42	1:1-2, 12-4	9:16-9, 22-7
Sat	6:43-9	1:15-7	10:14-22

Week 24

Mon	7:1-10	2:1-8	11:17-26, 33
Tues	7:11-7	3:1-13	12:12-4, 27-31
Wed	7:31-5	3:14-6	12:31-13:13
Thur	7:36-50	4:12-6	15:1-11
Fri	8:1-3	6:2-12	15:12-20
Sat	8:4-15	6:13-6	15:35-7, 42-9

Week 25

		Ezra	**Proverbs**
Mon	8:16-8	1:1-6	3:27-34
Tues	8:19-21	6:7-8, 12, 14-20	21:1-6, 10-3
Wed	9:1-6	9:5-9	30:5-9
		Haggai	**Qoheleth** (*Ecclesiastes*)
Thur	9:7-9	1:1-8	1:2-11
Fri	9:18-22	1:15-2:9	3:1-11
		Zechariah	
Sat	9:43-5	2:5-9, 14-5	11:9-12:8

Week 26

			Job
Mon	9:46-50	8:1-8	1:6-22
Tues	9:51-6	8:20-3	3:1-3, 11-7, 20-3
		Nehemiah	
Wed	9:57-62	2:1-8	9:1-13, 14-6
Thur	10:1-12	8:1-12	19:21-7
		Baruch	
Fri	10:13-6	1:15-22	38:1, 12-21; 40:3-5
Sat	10:17-24	4:5-12, 27-9	42:1-3, 5-6, 12-7

Week 27

		Jonah	**Galatians**
Mon	10:25-37	1:1-2:1, 11	1:6-12
Tues	10:38-42	3:1-10	1:13-24
Wed	11:1-4	4:1-11	2:1-2, 7-14
		Malachi	
Thur	11:5-13	3:13-20	3:1-5
		Joel	
Fri	11:15-26	1:13-5; 2:1-2	3:7-14
Sat	11:27-8	4:12-21	3:22-9

Week 28

		Romans	
Mon	11:29-32	1:1-7	4:22-4, 26-7, 31-5:1

Tues	11:37-41	1:16-25	5:1-6
Wed	11:42-6	2:1-11	5:18-25
			Ephesians
Thur	11:47-54	3:21-30	1:1-10
Fri	12:1-7	4:1-8	1:11-4
Sat	12:9-12	4:13, 16-8	1:15-23
Week 29			
Mon	12:13-21	4:20-5	2:1-10
Tues	12:35-8	5:12, 15, 17-21	2:12-22
Wed	12:39-48	6:12-8	3:2-12
Thur	12:49-53	6:19-23	3:14-21
Fri	12:54-9	7:18-25	4:1-6
Sat	13:1-9	8:1-11	4:7-16
Week 30			
Mon	13:10-7	8:12-7	4:32-5:8
Tues	13:18-21	8:18-25	5:21-33
Wed	13:22-30	8:26-30	6:1-9
Thur	13:31-5	8:31-9	6:10-20
			Philippians
Fri	14:1-6	9:1-5	1:1-11
Sat	114:1, 7-11	11:1-2, 11-2, 25-9	1:18-26
Week 31			
Mon	14:12-4	11:19-36	2:1-4
Tues	14:15-24	12:5-16	2:5-11
Wed	14:25-33	13:3-10	2:12-8
Thur	15:1-10	14:7-12	3:3-8
Fri	16:1-8	15:14-21	3:17-4:1
Sat	16:9-15	16:3-9, 16, 22-7	4:10-9
Week 32			
		Wisdom	**Titus**
Mon	17:1-6	1:1-7	1:1-9
Tues	17:7-10	2:23-3:9	2:1-8, 11-4
Wed	17:11-9	6:1-11	3:1-7
			Philemon
Thur	17:20-5	7:22-8:1	7-20

			2 John	
Fri	17:26-37	13:1-9	4-9	
			3 John	
Sat	18:1-8	18:14-6; 19:6-9	5-8	
Week 33				
		1 Maccabees	**Apocalypse**	
Mon	18:35-43	1:10-5, 41-4, 54-7, 62-4	1:1-4; 2:1-5	
		2 Maccabees		
Tues	19:1-10	6:18-31	3:1-6, 14-22	
Wed	19:11-28	7:1, 20-31	4:1-11	
		1 Maccabees		
Thur	19:41-4	2:15-29	5:1-10	
Fri	19:45-8	4:36-7, 52-9	10:8-11	
Sat	20:27-40	6:1-13	11:4-12	
Week 34				
		Daniel		
Mon	21:1-4	1:1-6, 8-20	14:1-5	
Tues	21:5-11	2:31-45	14:14-9	
Wed	21:12-9	5:1-6, 13-4, 16-7, 23-8		15:1-4
Thur	21:20-8	6:12-28	18:1-2, 21-3; 19:1-3, 9	
Fri	21:29-33	7:2-14	20:1-4, 11-21:2	
Sat	21:34-6	7:15-27	22:1-7	

III THE PASTORAL AGENDA

The weekday lectionary is probably the least appreciated and least understood part of the whole liturgical renewal inspired by Vatican II. It is certainly the most under-used part of the lectionary, yet a moment's thought about what it offers any community that assembles daily for the Eucharist shows that it has enormous potential as a means of developing Christian memory and understanding. This is a great pastoral challenge to everyone concerned, and the first step in meeting the challenge is to see what a valuable resource this lectionary is. It was assumed by Vatican II that people using this lectionary would be able to benefit from a more structured approach to the whole of the scriptural memory in that they were already people who could gather daily, but having then provided the fare for their Table of the Word, it is a pity so few have realised what is on offer.

This Lectionary has suffered over the past decades from two great problems. First, it requires some input from someone – usually this means the presiding priest – to point out where in the cycles we are and what sort of text we are readings which could be as simple as saying 'We are now going to read from the Book of ... for the next two weeks and these readings reminds us ...' Otherwise, people just hear bit after bit after bit, and bits which seem to be without pattern or plan become meaningless and boring. And, many people experience these readings as 'boring'. However, it is a boredom that is easily dispelled. Second, partly due to a lack of appreciation of this Lectionary and the importance of keeping to it, and partly through ignorance asserting that it is so boring that anything is better than it, the cycles are often chopped up unnecessarily: in some places it is common that every time there is a memorial of a saint, then this lectionary is abandoned in favour of a few over-used snippets from the Common pools of readings for various occasions. Every time the cycles are so interrupted, it makes the plan of readings on the remaining days even more incomprehensible.

Anyone looking through the above table will see that this lectionary offers a host of opportunities for use as the structure for teaching within the community. That this is, on the whole, a lost and ignored opportunity is regrettable, not least as it was the regular exposition of Scripture from lectionaries that formed the very heart of all theology in the first centuries of the church. Those who laboured in the late 1960s to reform the shabby and virtually useless weekday Lectionary of the Tridentine Rite were very much aware of the wonderful opportunity for a deeper understanding of the church's faith they were producing. Alas, in most communities that work has fallen on stony ground.

When this Lectionary was put together no one ever thought that just a few years' later the situation would have arisen that in many communities the daily celebration of the Eucharist would have to be replaced by non-eucharistic celebrations (namely, a Liturgy of the Word followed by Holy Communion which has remained from an earlier celebration of the Eucharist) led by someone who is not a priest. Now that this has happened, this Lectionary is even more important, for its regular exploration of the memory of the church means that it can feed the community with the leader receiving minimal training. This is another challenge that communities must face.

Lastly, many people who cannot attend the daily celebration of the Eucharist desire a guide to give them 'an overview of the Bible'. I am often asked for such an overview and told that people have tried to 'just start at Genesis' (and luckily they soon realised that reading the Bible 'from cover to cover' simply does not work), or they tried picking bits and pieces but found that is not organised enough to give an overview, or they tried reading a particular book but found that the few interesting bits were lost in a mire of detail: the simple answer is to recommend this Lectionary. It has the coverage, yet it has trimmed the parts that are less than helpful in that rather heterogeneous bundle of ancient writings that make up the anthology we call 'the Bible'.

A Practical Point

In most assemblies the same reader reads the first reading, then the psalm, and then the gospel acclamation. Then the assembly moves into a different mode to listen to the gospel read by the president or a deacon. This unwittingly conveys the signal that reading, psalm and 'alleluia' form a unit, and then comes the gospel. The simplest way to avoid this, while helping the assembly to recognise the psalm as a prayerful response to the first reading is for the reader to announce to the group, as soon as she/he reaches the ambo: 'Now let us sit to listen to the reading and to respond in prayer in the psalm.' Pause. 'A reading from the book of …'. Then, after the psalm is finished, the reader announces: 'Let us now stand for the gospel' and then leads the assembly in the acclamation while the deacon or president moves from his chair to the ambo.

CHAPTER NINE

Other celebrations

The core underlying strategy of the lectionary for the Eucharist is to provide a coherent and suitable sequence of readings for (1) the seasons surrounding Christmas and Easter, and (2) the Sundays of Ordinary Time, and then (3) the weekdays of Ordinary Time. Providing readings for every other celebration is secondary and, to an extent, more haphazard in that one cannot study patterns except to note that there is an attempt to provide 'suitable' readings – in the sense of some point of connection between the day / event being celebrated and the readings. And, usually, in these other celebrations all the readings (whether from the Old Testament, the Psalms, the epistles, or the gospels) are linked in some way to the common 'theme' of the celebration.

THE VARIETIES OF OTHER CELEBRATIONS

These other celebrations can be grouped as follows:

1. *Annual celebrations*, which are linked to the calculation of Easter, but belong neither to the season of Easter nor to Ordinary Time. These are (1) Trinity Sunday; (2) The Body and Blood of Christ (Corpus Christi); and (3) the Feast of the Sacred Heart of Jesus. These form a class apart as they are often celebrated with great solemnity, and treated as if they ranked with the key days of the season of Easter.

2. *The annual cycle for the celebration of feast days.* We can divide this into several parts:
- Feasts of the Lord which occur on fixed days in the year: The

Presentation in the Temple (2 February); the Annunciation (25 March); and the Transfiguration (6 August).

- Feasts of the Blessed Virgin Mary which sometimes are linked to the seasons (e.g. Mary the Mother of God on 1 January) and sometimes separate (e.g. the Assumption on 15 August). We should not forget that there are several lesser-known feasts as well: for example, the Birthday of Mary on 8 September, or the Presentation of Mary in the Temple on 21 November.

- Saints' days – some of which are celebrated by the whole church, some by countries, some by dioceses, and some in only one or two buildings.

3. *Celebrations of the Eucharist for special events:* weddings and funerals are the most common, but we also have to think about other events that can be celebrated in the context of a celebration of the Eucharist such as a baptism or the blessing of an abbess.

4. *Celebrations based around particular themes in spirituality:* e.g. a 'votive Mass of the Sacred Heart', or focused on particular needs: e.g. a celebration that is a petition for a good harvest.

Questions
In the case of all these types of special celebration we have to ask three questions:
(1) Do they have readings of their own?
(2) Do they interrupt the sequence of readings in the seasons Christmas/Easter or Ordinary Time?
(3) What lies behind the decision for those readings?

Responses
1. Celebrations linked to Easter
These all have readings of their own that are based on the theo-logical content of the feast, and all the readings (Old Testament and/or epistle, and the gospel) are intended to supply back-ground to, or reflections upon, that content. The readings can only be understood in reference to the feast being celebrated.

2. *Feast Days*

- Feasts of the Lord: these feasts have special readings which relate to the aspect of the mystery of Christ being celebrated, and they are read in that context.

- Feasts of Mary: some of these have specific readings and others have optional readings which can be taken from the 'common' stock of readings with a Marian theme or the readings set out for the day can be used. The advantage of the latter course is that it stops the larger plan of the lectionary being interrupted.

- Feasts of Saints: very few of these feasts have obligatory readings, a few others have optional readings, while most merely could have special readings taken from the appropriate 'common' pools of readings if there is a specific reason why a saint's day be given extra solemnity in a particular place. However, because the 1982 printing of the lectionary made suggestions for each saint's day from the common pool, in many places whenever a saint's memorial is celebrated, the calendar of readings for Ordinary Time is interrupted with isolated readings. The lectionary never envisaged such a disruption of its carefully planned scheme of readings for weekdays. The basic rule is this: except for an exceptional reason (e.g. in a church building dedicated to that saint), one should never depart from the Ordinary Time readings. The genius of the lectionary is that if people are gathering to celebrate the Eucharist regularly on weekdays, then the gathering should be fed in a regular way at the Table of the Word.

3. *Special Events*

By the very nature of these celebrations these have their own readings, whose significance can only be understood with reference to the event being celebrated.

4. *Particular Themes*

It is always possible to find 'themed' readings in the selections given in the lectionary for Votive Masses and Masses for particular intentions. However, each of these takes place on a day in the year which has its own readings prescribed for it and it is the intention of the lectionary that these should not be departed from lightly. It is a sad fact that many priests have such little respect for the lectionary's core structure that they depart from the fixed readings without a thought! In such departures they invariably read the same readings again and again, establishing private sets of preferred texts, and destroying one of the core values that the lectionary is there to guard: the Word of God is bigger than our imaginations and can always surprise us – if we let it.

CHAPTER TEN

How much do we read?

'How much of the Bible is read in the liturgy' is one of the most frequently asked questions when there is a discussion of the nature or content of the Liturgy of the Word at the Eucharist. At first sight, it would appear to be a question that would admit of a very direct answer: one would just go through the lectionary – or indeed the lists of readings found in other chapters of this book – count up all the verses, subtract them from the total number of verses in the Bible, and work out a percentage! It would be a very boring job, but it seems it could be done. Then we would know just how much of the Bible is used by the Catholic Church in its liturgy. This is an important question for some people because they believe that having such information would answer criticisms from people who say things like 'Catholics do not accept the Bible.' Whether or not having some statistics would ever satisfy such critics of the church's approach to the texts of the Scriptures is, moreover, a matter of debate. Many such critics actually equate the Word of God with the collection of texts, whereas the Catholic position is that the living Word could never be contained in a lifeless thing such as a book. However, the question of just 'how much do we read' still keeps coming up.

Regrettably, there is no simple answer to this question and the method that I have outlined – and which has often been attempted by people seeking an answer to this question – simply does not work. The remainder of this chapter is dedicated to showing why that question cannot be answered, but in the course of the explanation some other important aspects of the nature of the entire Liturgy of the Word come into view.

The first reason why calculating 'how much we use' is impossible relates to the nature of the four gospels. They are made up of much shorter little episodes – a miracle, a healing, a little incident, a parable, a little bit of teaching that forms a unity even if set in a larger sermon (e.g. the Beatitudes which open the Sermon on the Mount) – most of which are shorter than the chapter divisions we use to locate items within the gospels. It is these shorter units that we use, for the most part, as the basis for the gospels we read at the Eucharist. So given that there are only 52 Sundays a year, there is a limit to how much of the gospels we can use (allowing that there are a few extra occasions each year which are equivalent to Sundays). And, it would be little use to have more than we have on any one Sunday as it would overload communication and make preaching far more difficult. Long experience has taught us, and a moment's reflection will confirm, that if more than one episode is used at a time, then there is too much to hear, to listen to, to think about, and to absorb. To deal with this fact that there are just so few Sunday 'slots' in a year, the Lectionary of 1970 decided on the three year cycle: we now have about 160 slots! So how much do we read? The answer is as much as we can absorb.

The second reason why we cannot simply count up how much scripture we use is that while the Eucharist may be the centre of the church's liturgy, it is not its only liturgy. This book is devoted to the lectionary for the liturgy of the Eucharist, but there is also the lectionary for the Liturgy of the Hours (where the Office of Readings alone uses about a chapter of scripture each day), and there are the lectionaries for all the other rites (Baptism, Reconciliation, Marriage), along with lectionaries for special occasions. While very few, clergy apart, ever hear all these readings, it is only when all this formal use of scripture in the liturgy of the church is taken into account that we could produce a statistic on use. However, while some of these liturgies are on-going, such as the Eucharist and the Liturgy of the Hours, day by day, others are regular such as celebrations of reconciliation, others only come up now and again. So how much do we use? It depends on how active you are in taking part in the whole of the liturgy of the Body of Christ.

CHAPTER ELEVEN

Figuring out Psalm Numbers

The Problem

Many people wonder why they hear a psalm being referred to by one number in one place, and another number (usually one out in sequence) in some other place. Here is an example: Someone hears a musician announce 'We shall now sing the Twenty-third Psalm, 'The Lord is my shepherd,' to the setting Crimmond' – yet she sees it in the Lectionary marked down as Ps 22. Another example is a reader taking down the reference to look up the reading at home, but while the Lectionary has Ps 48, when that number is looked up in a Bible at home '48' is linked to a different Psalm. This is often disconcerting. And, for many people it leaves a nagging feeling that there is something very complex going on here that they do not understand.

Explanation

In the Lectionary and Missal the numbers given to the Psalms follow that given in the Latin *Ordo Lectionum* which, being in Latin, naturally follows the Vulgate numeration.[1] The Vulgate numeration followed that of the Old Greek translation ('The Septuagint') as this was seen as 'the Psalter of the Church.' However, most modern books, apart from Catholic liturgical books, follow the numeration of the Hebrew text of the Psalter.

In the English-language Lectionary for the Eucharist, the translation of the Psalms follows a special translation made for liturgical purposes in the early 1960s known as 'The Grail

---

1. To find out the exact versions of the Vulgate that were used in setting out the *Ordo Lectionum*, see the *General Instruction on the Lectionary*, n. 119, fn. 123.

Version.'[2] This version uses the Septuagint/Vulgate numbers.

For convenience, here is a concordance of the two numeration systems:

Septuagint	Hebrew
1 – 8	1 - 8
9	9 - 10
10 - 112	11 - 113
113	114 - 115
114 - 115	116
116 - 145	117 - 146
146 - 147	147
148 - 150	148 - 150

2. This was published as *The Psalms, a new translation* (Collins, London 1963).

CHAPTER TWELVE

Names for Biblical Books

Over the centuries the Scriptures have been used in many languages: initially Hebrew and Greek, then in Aramaic and Syriac, then in Latin, and then in the spoken languages of Christians worldwide. However, the moves from Hebrew to Greek to Latin (in the last couple of centuries before the time of Jesus and the first four centuries after his time), and then in the period of the Reformation in the sixteenth century from either the original languages or from Latin, have caused a situation where there are several names for some of the books of the Old Testament and for one book of the New Testament. This frequently causes confusion because several of these names are very close or sound alike. Moreover, in the current edition of the Lectionary in English a decision was taken to use the forms of names used in Latin, rather than the names by which these books are most commonly known in English (whether in scriptural scholarship or in the printing of bibles).[1]

To help clear up this confusion, this table may help:

The Old Testament

In the Vulgate the two books of Samuel and the two books of the Kings are treated as a series of four books collectively known as 'the four Books of the Kings' – so, if you are looking at any very old Catholic translation you may find that system used.

1 Samuel = I Kings = I Regum
2 Samuel = II Kings = II Regum
1 Kings = III Kings = III Regum
2 Kings = IV Kings = IV Regum

---

1. See the *General Instruction on the Lectionary*, nn. 119-22 which allows for either usage, but the English-language compilers in the early 1980s opted for the Latin-based forms – a regrettable decision.

In older Catholic translations the Greek word for 'chronicle' was preserved as the name for the two books of Chronicles.

1 Chronicles = I Paralipomenon
2 Chronicles = II Paralipomenon

The two separate books of Ezra and Nehemiah were often treated as the first and second books of Esdras in older translations. Here there is an additional problem as there are still two other books known as III and IV Esdras (found in some Bibles) which adds to the confusion – those other books are not used in the Lectionary as their canonical status is uncertain for Catholics.

Ezra = I Esdras
Nehemiah = II Esdras

There are four books – all considered to be part of the canon of Scripture by Catholics and, therefore, used in the Lectionary – which have similar names, similar sounding names, or have been linked with the name of Solomon as some stage in history. These are:

Qoheleth = Ecclesiastes = The Book of the Preacher
Song of Songs = Song of Solomon = Canticle of Canticles = Canticle of Solomon = Canticum canticorum
The Book of Wisdom = Wisdom of Solomon = Sapientia
Sirach = Ben Sira = the Wisdom of Sirach = Ecclesiasticus

The ones that cause most confusion in the Lectionary are: first, Ecclesiastes (pronounced: ek-clee-si-ass-tees) which is Qoheleth (pronounced: ko-hail-leth) and second Ecclesiasticus (pronounced: ek-clee-si-ass-tik-cus) which is Sirach.

New Testament
The Book of the Apocalypse = The Book of Revelation = The Revelation of John the Divine

The Greek word for 'a revelation' is *apocalypsis*, so Catholics tend to just transliterate the name and call it 'The Apocalypse', while the churches of the Reformation tend to translate the name and refer to it as 'The Book of Revelation'. The reason for

adding John's name is that there are many similar books, all referred to by the title 'apocalypse' that have survived from the
early church. However, only this one, attributed to John, has
become part of 'the church's list' (i.e. the canon).

CHAPTER THIRTEEN

Different Bibles

The first Christians understood their religion in terms of 'the Scriptures' by which they meant the books they already held sacred as Jews, and these books continued to be held sacred by Christians as the Old Testament. However, the history of any religion is never simple and it is rarely neat.

We often refer to 'ancient Judaism' or 'Judaism at the time of Jesus' or 'Second-temple Judaism' as if it were a monolithic religion with great consistency in beliefs and practices. However, such monolithic and consistent understandings of any religion are usually no more than the convenient labels given to people by outsiders who simply want to put them into common boxes. Just think of the phrase 'Christians believe in …' when we know that there are so many forms of Christianity (some of which would not even call some 'Christians' their sisters and brothers). It is the same with the term 'Judaism' in the past: it is better to refer to the 'Judaisms that existed at the time of Jesus'. And while all these Judaisms held some books to be 'the Scriptures', the actual list (the Greek word for a 'list' is *kanon*) of those books varied widely from group to group. At one extreme there was Samaritan Judaism which only considered 'the Books of Moses' (i.e. Genesis, Exodus, Leviticus, Numbers, and Deuteronomy) to be 'Scripture'; while there were groups of Greek-speaking Jews in cities around the Mediterranean which considered the list to include books written in Greek as well as old books written in Hebrew (and translated into Greek) to be 'Scripture' – and it was these Greek-speaking communities that had the greatest influence on the early church as it was their Scriptures (known as the

Septuagint) that became the Old Testament of the church.[1] Hence, both western Catholics and eastern Orthodox place a great deal of emphasis on the Septuagint and have very large Old Testament canons.

However, shortly after the time of Jesus there was a movement within Palestinian Judaism to restrict the list of books that would be considered Scripture to those they believed were originally written in Hebrew. That decision by the rabbis after Jesus's time led St Jerome (c. 342-420) to suspect the other books that Christians were reading in the liturgy were not 'really' canonical, and prompted a sharp reply from St Augustine (354-430) in his book *De doctrina christiana* that the canon of the church was determined by the usage of the churches rather than by the original language of the book concerned. However, the confusion had already set in and subsequent generations in the west continued to worry about the problem. This became even more problematic at the time of the Reformation when there was a new respect for Jerome as a scholar and a new set of suspicions of some of the books written in Greek as they were seen to support doctrines (e.g. purgatory) that the Protestants rejected.

The up-shot of all this is two-fold:

First, there is often an ecumenical problem over some of the books that Catholics and Orthodox consider canonical.

Second, when one buys a Bible, there is often considerable variation in the contents of the Old Testament section and hence there are often 'Catholic versions', 'common versions' and so forth.

The whole topic of 'canonicity' is too complex to examine here.[2] Put simply, the problem is that 'the Scriptures' never came with a 'contents page' and so Christians often worry about

---

1. For a detailed guide to this whole question see M. Hengel, *The Septuagint as Christian Scripture, Its Prehistory and the Problem of its Canon* (trs M. E. Biddle, Edinburgh 2002); and A. Wasserstein and D. J. Wasserstein, *The Legend of the Septuagint from Classical Antiquity to Today* (Cambridge 2006).

2. For a detailed account, see B. M. Metzger, *The Canon of the New Testament: Its Origin, Development, and Significance* (Oxford 1987).

whether the canon is 'a list of inspired books' or 'an inspired list of books' – think about it, there is a world of a difference between the two notions. The topic was so disputed at the time of the Reformation that the Council of Trent tried to solve the question for the purposes of the liturgy, for the group that were still in communion with Rome, by setting out an official list of books, but even this did not solve all the questions for there were a few books (e.g. III and IV Esdras) which Trent was not willing to say were on the list (because Trent followed Augustine and he had not mentioned them) but, equally, they were not willing to have them disappear (so Trent ordered that they be printed in Latin Bibles *ut ne pereant*, 'lest they disappear altogether').[3]

This table shows the contents of the various 'lists' of the books of the Old Testament (there is no equivalent dispute about the contents of the New Testament) as they are found in printed bibles:

	1	2	3	4	5	6	7	8	9	10	11	12	13
Genesis	•	•	•	•	•	•	•	•	•	•	•	•	•
Exodus	•	•	•	•	•	•	•	•	•	•	•	•	•
Leviticus	•	•	•	•	•	•	•	•	•	•	•	•	•
Numbers	•	•	•	•	•	•	•	•	•	•	•	•	•
Deuteronomy	•	•	•	•	•	•	•	•	•	•	•	•	•
Joshua	•	•	•	•	•	•	•	•	•	•	•	•	•
Judges	•	•	•	•	•	•	•	•	•	•	•	•	•
Ruth	•	•	•	•	•	•	•	•	•	•	•	•	•
1 Samuel	•	•	•	•	•	•	•	•	•	•	•	•	•
2 Samuel	•	•	•	•	•	•	•	•	•	•	•	•	•
1 Kings	•	•	•	•	•	•	•	•	•	•	•	•	•
2 Kings	•	•	•	•	•	•	•	•	•	•	•	•	•
1 Chronicles	•	•	•	•	•	•	•	•	•	•	•	•	•
2 Chronicles	•	•	•	•	•	•	•	•	•	•	•	•	•
Ezra	•	•	•	•	•	•	•	•	•	•	•	•	•
Nehemiah	•	•	•	•	•	•	•	•	•	•	•	•	•

---

3 However, while these books *ut ne pereant* are always printed in Bibles in Latin, most Catholic Bibles in modern languages do not include them.

	1	2	3	4	5	6	7	8	9	10	11	12	13
Tobit	•		•			•	•	•	•	•	•	•	•
Judith	•		•			•	•	•	•	•	•	•	•
Esther 1-10	•	•	•	•	•	•	•	•	•	•	•	•	•
Esther 10-16	•		•			•	•	•		•	•	•	•
Job	•	•	•	•	•	•	•	•	•	•	•	•	•
Psalms	•	•	•	•	•	•	•	•		•	•	•	•
Psalms of Solomon			•										
Proverbs	•	•	•	•	•	•	•	•	•	•	•	•	•
Qoheleth	•	•	•	•	•	•	•	•	•	•	•	•	•
Song of Songs	•	•	•	•	•	•	•	•	•	•	•	•	•
Wisdom of Solomon	•		•			•	•	•		•	•	•	•
Odes of Solomon			•										
Sirach	•		•			•	•	•		•	•	•	•
Isaiah	•	•	•	•	•	•	•	•	•	•	•	•	•
Jeremiah	•	•	•	•	•	•	•	•	•	•	•	•	•
Lamentations	-(?)	•	•	•	•	•	•	•	•	•	•	•	•
Baruch	-(?)		•			•	•	•		•	•	•	•
Letter of Jeremiah	-(?)		•		-	-	-		-	-	-	-	•
Ezekiel	•	•	•	•	•	•	•	•	•	•	•	•	•
Daniel	•	•	•	•	•	•	•	•	•	•	•	•	•
Prayer of Azariah	-		•		-	-	-		-	-	-		
Bel and the Dragon	-		•		-	-	-		-	-	-	•	•
Susanna	-		•		-	-	-		-	-	-	•	•
Hosea	•	•	•	•	•	•	•	•	•	•	•	•	•
Joel	•	•	•	•	•	•	•	•	•	•	•	•	•
Amos	•	•	•	•	•	•	•	•	•	•	•	•	•
Obadiah	•	•	•	•	•	•	•	•	•	•	•	•	•
Jonah	•	•	•	•	•	•	•	•	•	•	•	•	•
Micah	•	•	•	•	•	•	•	•	•	•	•	•	•
Nahum	•	•	•	•	•	•	•	•	•	•	•	•	•
Habakkuk	•	•	•	•	•	•	•	•	•	•	•	•	•
Zephaniah	•	•	•	•	•	•	•	•	•	•	•	•	•
Haggai	•	•	•	•	•	•	•	•	•	•	•	•	•

	1	2	3	4	5	6	7	8	9	10	11	12	13
Zachariah	•	•	•	•	•	•	•	•	•	•	•	•	•
Malachi	•	•	•	•	•	•	•	•	•	•	•	•	•
1 Maccabees	•			•			•	•	•	•	•	•	•
2 Maccabees	•			•			•	•	•	•	•	•	•
3 Maccabees				•								•	
4 Maccabees				•								•	
1 (III) Esdras				•				*				•	•
2 (IV) Esdras								*				•	•
Ps 151				•				*				•	
Prayer of Manassah				•				*				•	•

Key to Table

1. Canon recognised by Augustine in *De doctrina christiana* 2, 8,13; he states there are 44 books in the OT – there is no mention of Lamentations-Baruch.

2. Canon Jerome believed to the the *'hebraica veritas'*.

3. The Septuagint Canon as found in printed editions.

4. The Hebrew Canon as found in printed editions.

5. The Canon of Martin Luther's printed edition in German.

6. The Latin Vulgate as prescribed by the Council of Trent (NB the books *'ut ne pereant'*).

7. The Canon of the Council of Trent.

8. The Canon of the Douai Version (1609).

9. The Canon of the Authorised Version (1611) (NB until early 19th century this was printed 'with the apocrypha').

10. RSV – Catholic Edition (1957).

11. The Jerusalem Bible (ET – 1966).

12. New Revised Standard Version (1989).

13. Revised English Version (1989).

Symbols:

- = incorporated into preceeding work

* = those books which Trent did not consider canonical but which it wished printed in an appendix to the Vulgate *'ut ne pereant'* ('lest they perish').

CHAPTER FOURTEEN

Concluding observations

Since as long as we have records of the contents of the readings used at the Eucharist, it has been the case that these have been prescribed, usually using a recognised formula, for each Sunday. Sometimes these Lectionaries (i.e. the lists of readings appointed for use on specific days) have been in special books (as we have them today), sometimes the readings have been in-corporated with the other texts for the Eucharist (as in the missal of 1570), and sometimes these have just been lists of references that then had to be looked up in copies of the Scriptures. However, many people today wonder about the value of having a Lectionary and some suggest that it would be better if the choice of readings was left to either the congregation, or a spe-cial group within the gathering, or even to the preacher or the president of the assembly. This seems, indeed, a trivial matter. After all, a preacher might have a special message that he be-lieves needs to be heard and could pick passages accordingly. A gathering might have some special circumstances that might make a particular text either especially appropriate or inappro-priate. And, there is the fact that many of the churches of the Reformation rejected Lectionaries as limitations on freedom, yet were far more interested in the Scriptures than Catholics.

All these points have a certain validity and all appear fre-quently when there are discussions about the Liturgy of the Word. So, for example, at a special gathering for a specific group or special event, there is often a very good case to be made for choosing readings that relate to that group's situation or their special event. However, there is an important distinction to be made between such special gatherings and the normal weekly gathering of the community for the Eucharist. Special events and special groups are precisely that: special, and out-of-the-ordinary. But the community becomes the Body of Christ when it gathers as just that: the community of all the baptised assembling each week to celebrate not some special event, but their on-going relationship with God over the course of the liturgical year.

Therefore, in this chapter we want to address three questions:

- What is the purpose of a Lectionary?
- What is the value of a Lectionary?
- What are the challenges for us who use the Lectionary?

THE PURPOSE OF A LECTIONARY

There are four main reasons why we use a Lectionary. Two of these can be seen as 'practical' – relating to the situation we find ourselves in as human beings gathering publicly and regularly – and two can be seen as 'theological' – relating to the specific activity of being disciples gathered for the Eucharist. Let us start with the practical reasons:

1. Avoiding being at the mercy of whims

The simplest, and most obvious, reason for having a Lectionary is that we all have bits of the memory of the church – as represented by the Scriptures – that we like, other bits we dislike, and other bits we simply find un-moving or uninteresting. I have often heard people say 'I don't like John['s gospel], he is so difficult to understand!' and without a Lectionary, that would be the end of John's witness to Jesus for such a person. Equally, it is a common belief that 'The Beatitudes' (Mt 5:3-12) is the most accessible and best loved text in the four gospels. Between these extremes there are all the various ways of picking particular biblical texts and making them the centre around which a whole theology can revolve. In that situation, the community would hear a handful of texts again and again, while the larger sweep of the gospel would be lost.

Such a reduction of the Christian message to a handful of catchphrases has occurred time and again in Christian history, but the presence of a formula setting out as wide a range of readings as possible is a defence against it. Because there is a Lectionary, we are taken away from our private concerns and made confront the texts we like with those we dislike, the texts we find attractive along with those we find difficult and challenging. It is because the Lectionary, by its distance from how we feel on a particular day, can challenge us to move out of our private concerns and our momentary attitudes that we should always be very slow to change from the readings set out for a certain day on the assumption that 'our choice is more relevant'.

2. Avoiding having the liturgy made into propaganda

It might sound far fetched, but without a Lectionary a community gathered for the Eucharist would be at the mercy of whatever message someone, the priest, the local bishop, the civil authorities, might wish to reinforce at the Eucharist by either picking or rejecting certain readings. Imagine the furore that could be caused at the time of an election if certain texts were used in such a way that they could be seen to support one side or another. Over the years this desire for the church to preach the right message has been a concern of many governments; the presence of a Lectionary removes the temptation to meddle. The formation of the community of the church is an on-going process that should not be diverted to this or that 'cause'.

3. Respecting the nature of the gospels

A less obvious, but even more important reason for avoiding a 'picking the nice bits' policy is that each gospel was preached as a unity: each is a particular way of remembering the words and work of the Christ. To just pick and mix does not respect the internal nature of the four individual gospels, whereas the semi-continuous reading of the gospels, along with Christmas and Easter, over a three-year cycle does try to give each evangelist a voice. No selection of readings is perfect, but today more of the four texts is heard by the average congregation on Sunday than at any time in the past 1500 years.

4. Respecting the nature of the Liturgy of the Word

We now come to the most important reason for a Lectionary: when we gather for the Eucharist, we are the Body of Christ, but we are also just one member of the whole Body worldwide. Our unity as Christians, our unity in Jesus Christ, is expressed in the unity of the Liturgy of the Word throughout the whole church on that day. The Liturgy of the Word at the Sunday Eucharist is not just a few bits and pieces of pious memory that can form the basis of a bit of teaching: it is a sacred moment, the school of the Holy Spirit in which Christ is present in his word and leads us towards the Father. The Liturgy of the Word is the property of the whole church, just as the Liturgy of the Eucharist is the property of the whole Church. Because this liturgy is one of the presences of the Christ, it has an intrinsic unity: in those readings each day the Spirit is turning texts into the Word of God. We are worldwide one people, seeking to live as sisters and brothers, and we have a unity in listening and then in prayer as a priestly people in the Prayer of the Faithful each Sunday.

This view of the Liturgy of the Word, and therefore of the place of the Lectionary within it, is based on our view of the role of the Holy Spirit in the church. The church is the body inspired, given life, by the Spirit, 'the giver of life'. It is within the whole church, manifested in the local church, that the Spirit's action of revealing to us Jesus as the Son of the Father takes place. The gospels, and all the scriptures, are the inheritance of the whole community, and it is as a whole community, gathered in the Spirit, we gather to hear again the Word each Sunday.

THE VALUE OF THE LECTIONARY

Of all the books produced during the restoration of the liturgy inspired by Vatican II, the Lectionary seems to be one that draws fire from all quarters in the Catholic Church at present.

So-called 'conservatives' attack it simply on the grounds that they imagine some gilded age – a slippery moment in real time – prior to the new Order of Mass in the vernacular. In those days they did not have to be distracted by readings, they argue, and could concentrate on their prayers. But they fail to point out that this was mainly because the readings were in Latin and so could not be understood by the majority of the congregation; while at a Low Mass (i.e. the ordinary rite used on all but a couple of oc-casions each year) they were read facing away from the congreg-ation in a low voice and so could not be heard even by those who knew Latin, unless they had remarkable hearing. So-called 'liberals' attack the Lectionary as they claim they would like readings with 'relevance to today' – an equally slippery moment in the human historical continuum. What is 'relevant' to some-one today will be seen as concentration on the 'ephemeral' to-morrow. Between these groups lie many preachers / celebrants / readers who criticise it for (1) giving too many readings; (2) readings which are 'difficult' to preach upon; (3) readings which do not 'make sense' (e.g. do not have a readily recognisable 'theme'); (4) readings which do not provide a 'thought for the day'; (5) any Old Testament readings included at all; or (6) the gospels do not fit with 'the epistles' (i.e. the second readings). Hopefully, most of these criticisms will be addressed some-where in this book or, at least, some pointers given as to how they should be addressed.

By amazing contrast, outside the Catholic Church the Lectionary seems to be winning more friends by the day. Churches that are familiar with the notion of a Lectionary and a liturgical year who want to up-date their Lectionary are often opting for the Roman Lectionary – restyled 'the common lec-tionary' – as their working base because they think that it is as good as any such work is likely to be. Other churches either dis-covering the value of a liturgical year or of using a Lectionary, or both, are coming to it as if it were a preaching tool of excellence. And, a few lections from the Catholic canon apart,[1] the

1. See the previous chapter for more detail.

Lectionary has been adopted as it stands, usually not out of some vague desire for ecumenical conformity – a typically Catholic concern – but because of its intrinsic worth. The simple facts are, firstly, that without Lectionaries any celebrant/worship leader is likely to fall back on a canon within the canon of 'pet texts' and the breadth of the Christian memory is curtailed; and, second, given the content of the Christian canon any attempt to create a broad Lectionary is going to involve compromises, swings and roundabouts, and will always leave some loose ends. But as Lectionaries go, the 1970 Lectionary appears to be as good as anyone can come up with at the moment if that Lectionary is for use in a community where the Eucharist is the norm for a Sunday gathering. Given that the Lectionary was created in just a few liturgically busy years in the late 1960s, this is a great tribute to its creators.

No Lectionary – since it must be a work of compromises – will ever be free of critics; but justice demands that if we accept the basic liturgical premises that have inspired Christian reading at the Eucharist since at least the early second century, then we should acknowledge our Lectionary as about as good as any rite within the whole of Christian liturgy has ever had. My own view is that it is not only as good as any, but I know of none better in the last 1800 years for which we have evidence in Greek, Syriac, and Latin. Yet, to date, its genuine exploitation in the formation of Christian consciousness is minimal.

Lastly, if one consequence of the excellence of the Lectionary has been its adoption by others outside the Roman rite or even any connection with Rome, then this is a fact that must now be a factor in the thought of anyone brashly calling for a new or different Lectionary. It could be that if the Roman rite were to change its Sunday Lectionary unilaterally, it would be, by that change, actually sundering an emerging unity in Christian worship – a unity created by groups recognising in this Lectionary an encapsulation of their view of Scripture's place in worship.

1. *Valuing the Lectionary*

The notion that the readings prescribed for the celebration of the Eucharist on a particular day should normally form the basis of the homily is an idea that it relatively new.[2] It is an idea that was familiar to St Augustine (354-430) and those before him, but one that disappeared from sight shortly after his time and did not re-emerge in the Catholic Church until the Second Vatican Council. It represents a new awareness of the nature of the Word of God in the liturgy, and a different appreciation of the place of the liturgy in the life of the community and the spirituality of individuals from that which went before. This new understanding is taking far longer to 'bed in' within the life of the church than those who pioneered the restoration of the Liturgy of the Word in the 1960s ever imagined it would take.

The simple fact is that, for the most part, we have not really taken this change in our understanding of the Liturgy of the Word to heart.

- Priests ordained before 1970 were not trained for this situation and adapted to it often without adequate training. There were many other things to be re-learned as part of the introduction of the new Rite of Mass.

- Many seminaries re-structured their courses in Scripture after Vatican II to bring them into line with the scholarly study of Scripture, but while this was a much-needed development it is not the same as training people to use the Lectionary as the basis of training. Many priests believe because they are good at Scripture that they know how to appreciate the Lectionary; others think that because they are good communicators they understand the link between the Lectionary and their preaching.

- While there have been massive strides made to train readers in most communities, this has usually focused on the technical skills of voice-projection, reading aloud, and using the

---

2. See the *General Instruction on the Lectionary*, nn. 24-7 for details.

microphones well. The background preparation is often non-existent.

- There is continued tendency in every matter concerned with the Eucharist to devote far more energy to the 'Liturgy of the Eucharist' than to the 'Liturgy of the Word'. This concentration on the 'Liturgy of the Eucharist' continues unwittingly a dismissive attitude to what was, prior to Vatican II, referred to as 'the Fore-mass' or the 'Mass of the Catechumens' and was, in effect, seen as only a preliminary to 'the real thing'. One finds this attitude at every level of the Catholic Church: in parishes there are days of reflection and training for 'Ministers of the Eucharist' and special dedication ceremonies, but the 'readers' are just left to get on with it. In the Code of Canon Law there are umpteen canons dealing with the Eucharist, but not one of those regulations is directed to the Liturgy of the Word at the Eucharist.

It is a sorry state that often means that the people are rejecting the Lectionary willy-nilly, and either dropping readings, or substituting their own choices of scriptural readings or bits and pieces that cannot be said to belong to the core of the common tradition that unites us as the Body of Christ.

2. Sexist language

One other problem that crops up whenever readers gather to discuss their ministry or the church's use of the Scriptures in the liturgy is the issue of male-centred language: the use of 'man' when we mean 'human' and 'his' or 'him' when the context could equally be 'her/his' or 'her/him'. When this question of inclusive language is raised, some people simply dismiss it as a 'fad', and then argue that 'it is only a matter of words.' This defensive reaction always annoys me for two reasons: first, to dismiss the question as only 'a matter of words' forgets that we are there using words, words, and more words to help us celebrate the revelation of God. To dismiss words so flippantly hides, I suspect, a belief that the whole Liturgy of the Word which depends on words is not really all that important after all. Second, for many people, and they are not only women, the use of non-inclusive language is deeply offensive and is a form of offence that they no longer have to endure in many aspects of life that have less reason to be sensitive to people's sense of self-worth than the liturgy. The simple fact is that we have a problem; and every time we read a lection that contains obviously gender-exclusive language, there will be some people listening who will be upset and will have been alienated rather than inspired by what they have heard.

What can be done about this? The lectionary in common use was produced in the early 1980s before it was realised by many people that this was a serious issue. Since then there have been several statements about the issue where various bishops have argued that even if there is a new Lectionary, changing to inclusive language would not be allowed as this would not be 'faithful to the Latin' or some such similar argument. Whether or not such arguments have any validity is not my concern here, but the prognosis is not good that we will get an inclusive language edition any time soon. However, some communities, or individual readers who are offended by having to read what they consider sexist language, have come up with several work-arounds. In some places they use the Anglican version of the Lectionary on these days (the Anglicans took over most of the Lectionary but use an inclusive language version). In other communities, the liturgy group prints out a copy of the reading from an electronic version of an inclusive-language translation (e.g. the New Revised Standard Version) to which they have access. In other places they have altered the text by hand in the Lectionary. And, lastly there are readers who whenever they meet sexist language silently change the text, alter the offending words, without comment. This is a serious issue: it is a matter that should be discussed openly when readers meet, it should be addressed each week by liturgy planning groups, and then one of the simple remedies adopted.

And finally ...

The Lectionary represents to us over the course of the liturgy's cycles the core of the gospel in terms of the preaching of the church since the days of the first apostles. It demands from us not just competence in the study of the Scriptures, but an equal competence in theology to appreciate them not simply as texts but within the memory of the church. This task of appreciating our Lectionary has barely begun – it will be a work that may take generations.

CHAPTER FIFTEEN

Further Reading

The first step in gaining a deeper understanding of the Lectionary is to read the *General Instruction on the Lectionary* which can be found printed as the introduction to the first volume of the actual Lectionary book used at the liturgy. Once this has been studied, one can move on to more detailed books and articles on the Lectionary as such, and on the readings.

A good, quick introduction to the notion of a Lectionary can be found in the article 'Lectionaries' by Horace T. Allen, Jr in *The New SCM Dictionary of Liturgy and Worship*, edited by Paul F. Bradshaw (London 2002), pp. 274-7. While if you want to examine the history of the Lectionary, you should read Eric Palazzo, *A History of Liturgical Books from the Beginning to the Thirteenth Century* (Collegeville, MN, 1998), pp. 83-105 and 149-60.

To study the content of the present liturgy, in terms of its overall structure, the most convenient work is Norman Bonneau, *The Sunday Lectionary: Ritual Word, Paschal Shape* (Collegeville, MN, 1998).

If, however, the most pressing problem when reading is not knowing the context from which a particular reading is taken, then there are several good reference works on the Scriptures which can easily be consulted. The most convenient one-volume commentary on the whole of the Scriptures, and covering all the background topics also, is the *New Jerome Biblical Commentary* (edited by R. E. Brown, J. A. Fitzmyer, and R. E. Murphy, London 1989) – it is not a work of the faint-hearted, but it is thorough main-stream scholarship. On a smaller scale there are umpteen 'Bible dictionaries' and a reliable, easy-to-use, and up-to-date dictionary is *Eerdmans Dictionary of the Bible* (edited by David Noel Freedman, Grand Rapids, MI, 2000).

However, when our memories are recalled in the context of the Eucharist, we do so not simply in order to identify who we are as the People of God, but as a basis for our gathering in union with the Lord to offer a thanksgiving sacrifice to the Father. The whole celebration of the Eucharist is, therefore, more important than any of its parts. If you want to investigate the readings as presented for the Eucharistic gathering on a particular day, then there are many guides providing materials for liturgy groups and preachers, but which usually have commentaries on the readings. I have produced a series of books for Advent-Christmas, Lent-Easter, and one for each year of Ordinary Time entitles *Liturgical Resources for* ... (published by the publishers of this book), but there are many such works available.

The question of inclusive language has generated a great deal of discussion in recent years, much of which is little informed by scholarship. For a good basic study of this complex topic, look at Gail Ramshaw, *Worship: Searching for Language* (Washington, DC 1988).

By the same author

The Liturgical Resources Series

Veritable treasure troves of extra resources, insights and practical suggestions for the liturgy of every Sunday and major feast-day of the three-year cycle. Resources for the seasons come in two volumes, *Liturgical Resources for Lent and Easter* and *Liturgical Resources for Advent and Christmastide*. Resources for the Sundays of Ordinary time come in separate volumes for each of the three years (The year of Mark is due in autumn 2008).

For each occasion, Fr O'Loughlin offers:

(a) A Celebrant's Guide which covers Introduction to the Celebration, Penitential Rite, Headings for the Readings, Prayer of the Faithful, Eucharistic Prayers (suggestions for Prefaces etc), Invitation to the Our Father, Sign of Peace, Invitation to Communion, Communion Reflection, Dismissal.

(b) Commentaries on each of the readings and psalms.

(c) Homily Notes.

Available from your usual supplier
or direct from Columba on the Order Form overleaf

ORDER FORM

Quant	ISBN	Title	Euro	Sterling
	9781856075930	Liturgical Resources Year A (Matthew)	€18.99	£13.50
	9781856075596	Liturgical Resources Year C (Luke)	€14.99	£9.99
	9781856075541	Liturgical Resources Advent & Christmas	€14.99	£9.99
	9781856074780	Liturgical Resources Lent & Easter	€14.99	£9.99

Sub-Total _____

Postage & Packing _____

Total _____

Please add 15% for postage and packing to a max of €10.00/£7.00. Overseas customers please apply for rates. All prices are quoted in euro and sterling but are subject to change without notification.

Name _____

Address _____

Tel _____ E-mail _____

Payment options

❑ Please charge to my VISA / ACCESS card number:

_____

Expiry Date _____ Signature _____

Security Code (last 3 digits on back of card) _____

❑ I enclose Cheque/postal order for €/£ _____

Return to your usual supplier or direct to:
The Columba Press
55A Spruce Avenue, Stillorgan Industrial Park,
Blackrock, Co. Dublin, Ireland
Tel: + 353 (0)1 294 2560 Fax: + 353 (0)1 294 2564
E-mail: sales@columba.ie Web: www.columba.ie

❑ Please tick if you wish to receive our e-mail newsletter with exclusive special offers and information on all our new titles. (You can also sign up to our mailing list on www.columba.ie)